PAGAN FIRE SEMINARS
Private Practice to Public Ritual

From Private Practice To Public Ritual:
Ritual Foundations I
February 2012

Blacklick Woods Metropark
Beech-Maple Shelter
Columbus, OH

Edition 1.0.1

Copyright © 2012
Three Cranes Grove, ADF
PO Box 3264
Columbus, OH 43210

Please visit us at:

http://www.threecranes.org/
http://www.adf.org/

and see more of our publications at:
http://www.lulu.com/garanus

Content created by:

Rev. Michael J Dangler
Rev. James "Seamus" Dillard
Rev. Kirk Thomas
Melissa S. Burchfield

Cover photo by Sarah-Jayne Chapman, ©2011
Cover design by Rev. James "Seamus" Dillard

Parts of this book are featured in other works:

"Understanding Ritual," Under the heading, "Understanding Sacrifice" is Rev. Kirk Thomas' paper, "The Nature of Sacrifice."

"Exercises for Building Personal Ritual Work", particularly under the headings "Speaking in Ritual" and "Movement in Ritual" are large parts of Rev. Kirk Thomas' paper, "The Well-Trained Ritualist." Parts also appear under "Memorization" in the section, "Additional Work."

"Developing Group Rituals," under the heading, "Circles of Concentration" is Rev. Kirk Thomas' paper, "Concentration in Ritual"

"Additional Work," under "Using Music Effectively in Ritual Space" is by Melissa S. Burchfield

Introduction 5
Understanding Ritual 7
Definitions 7
Understanding Sacrifice 8
Praying With a Good Fire 27
Personal Ritual Work 31
Learning to Cleanse and Purify 31
Building a Shrine 33
Writing Simple Prayers 35
Developing Personal Rituals 41
Making the Commitment 41
Center and Circumference 47
Crossing the Boundaries, Painting the Cosmos 50
Finding Focus 53
Divination and Omen-Taking 58
Ritual Clothing, Jewelry, and Props 61
Blessing Your Tools 63
Keys to Props and Locations 65
Summary of Ritual Props 66
Exercises for Building Personal Ritual Work 67
Speaking in Ritual 68
Movement in Ritual 83
Developing Group Rituals 85
Prayer in Public Spaces 85

- Building Group Cohesion 86
- Circles of Concentration 87
- Being a Leader, Being a Follower 96
- Articulating Ritual Vision 99
- Creating a Script 100
- Understanding Space 106

Additional Work *113*
- Memorization 113
- Improvisation 116
- Using Music Effectively in Ritual Space 118
- Preparing For the Unexpected 123
- Meditation for Groups 126
- Ritual Criticism and Review 129

Recipes From Skarlett *132*
- Chicken-Cheddar Potato Pie 132
- Spiced Meat Pie 133

Further Reading *134*

Introduction

Do you give good ritual?

It may sound trite, but the central question being asked is not at all uncommon: the act of building a good working ritual group is dependent on projecting an air of competent, skilled ritual work.

What many people do not realize is that good ritual begins at home, in front of your shrine, where you are not doing public work at all. The guidance and exercises in this book are aimed at building your private work, and then showing you how to expand that work into the public arena.

We were very fortunate to have a great group of folks for the seminar that kicked this off, titled the same as this book. The goals of that seminar and the goals of this book are the same:

1) Understanding what is going on in ritual
2) Deepening and developing your personal ritual work
3) Learning to apply personal work to public work
4) Developing skills specific to public work based on private work
5) Enriching your personal work with the joy of public work

To do this, we will focus on five primary steps that we hope will benefit you as you begin to deepen your ritual work:

1) **Build a fire in your heart** that burns brightly through prayer, offering and blessing.
2) **Feed that fire** with practice and exercises. Brighten it by sharpening your skills.
3) **Share that fire** with others. Show them what it looks like to have a fire within you.
4) **Light the fire** in others: teach others to kindle the fire in their own hearts, and share the flame of your devotion with them.
5) **Learn to draw the flames together** to brighten the world and the cosmos.

We would like to extend special thanks to Rev. Kirk Thomas, Archdruid of Ár nDraíocht Féin: A Druid Fellowship (ADF); Missy Burchfield, Grove Bard of Three Cranes Grove, ADF, and everyone who came out to the seminar in Feb. 2012: all of you made this possible.

A Brief Outline:

The first chapter is likely the densest: it is about understanding the most basic concepts of our relationships with the Powers, and the idea of sacrifice. It also provides some very important details and definitions of terms that we will use throughout the book.

The second chapter really focuses on the basic tools that will build your work: basic prayer and creating sacred space.

The third chapter discusses expanding from prayer to ritual: once you have the basic tools, it is time to move to a broader devotion that will brighten the fire of piety within you. This chapter covers everything from taking omens to what to wear in ritual.

The fourth chapter is a sort of bridge between the personal and the public: it will focus on a couple of key things, speaking and acting, that you should use in your personal rites in order to understand the concepts as they apply to public ritual.

The fifth chapter is all about developing group rituals: working with others, understanding how prayer is different in front of or with a group, connecting with others in ritual, and some of the nuts and bolts about how to get your point across about what the heck you want to do.

The final chapter is all about additional work: skills that rarely enter our personal worship (memorization, improvisation, musical numbers, and criticism) that are very difficult to get a handle on when you start.

So, I hope that you enjoy the ride: we certainly enjoyed creating the book!

Understanding Ritual

What is ritual?
Note that "ritual" and "rite" are not defined in religious terms. We know that there are rites and ritual actions that have nothing to do with religion (civil ceremonies such as symbolic groundbreakings, the first pitch of the season in baseball, and graduations). Additionally, there are religions that have little to do with mystical or spiritual beings (such as Zen Buddhism). As a result, a definition of ritual is best removed from these things.

Don't let this chapter get you down: there are a lot of concepts here, and some of it will get you thinking in new ways about words you've used for a long time. You might consider it a "reference" chapter, and consider using it just for that when you hit a concept that doesn't seem to fit.

Definitions

Each book on ritual must begin with definitions, and this is no different. Here are some very basic definitions for words you will find throughout this book:

- **Rite** – Specific enactments in specific places and time, differentiated as something "other" than "ordinary" behavior, recognized by a cultural group, and are enacted by "ritualists" (persons engaging in ritual activity). Rites are often named (e.g. "midsummer rite" or "Samhain rite"), and are likely to be part of a broader ritual system or tradition that includes other rites as well. From Latin, *ritus*, related to Greek *arithmos*, "number."

- **Ritual** – A general idea of which rites are specific instances. You do not do "a ritual" or "several rituals." You do "a rite" or "several rites." Ritual is a formal division or characterization, rather than something enacted. To "do ritual" or "study ritual" is to do or study classes of rites. We will speak of "ritual" in general and "rites" in specific.

- **Liturgy** – A public rite or a general term for public ritual. The word has connotations of service to others, with the original word meaning "public service" and "liturgist" effectively meaning "public servant." From Greek *leitourgiā*, "public service", related to the PIE root ***werg-***, "work." There is no such thing as a "solitary liturgy."

- **Sacrifice** – The act of making something sacred. Our working definition of sacrifice is "to set something apart from ordinary reality." Latin *sacer*, "sacred," + *facere*, "to make" or "to do." Sacrifice is any act or ritual that sets apart or consecrates items or gifts to another being.

- **Offering** – Offerings are things given, both physical and non-physical. The difference between the broad concept of offering and the narrower concept of sacrifice may be said to reside in the fact that a rite is part of sacrifice. In other words, offerings are given, but the sacrifice is the sum of actions taken on those offerings.

- **Religion** – Primarily a western concern, the definition of religion is complicated, but it can best be said to be those practices done, beliefs held, and vision of the cosmos seen by an individual or group. The aim of religion appears to be "re-binding" a person to that which they hold sacred. From Latin *re-*, *"again"* + *ligāre*, "to bind, tie." **"Personal Religion,"** then, is the act of building and re-building these connections in ways that empower your personal sense of the sacred.

Understanding Sacrifice

We know what ritual is: now, what are we doing when we do ritual? The most common thing that we do is make sacrifice unto the beings we honor.

When modern people use the word "sacrifice" today, they usually mean something negative and uncomfortable, such as when we refer to the "ultimate sacrifice" when speaking about the deaths of our soldiers in war. But the word had a quite different meaning in the religious lives of the ancients.

The word "sacrifice" comes from two Latin roots, *sacer*, meaning "sacred," and *facere*, meaning "to make" or "to do." So sacrifice would mean, "to make sacred" in this context.

The word "sacred" probably comes from the Proto-Indo-European (PIE) word **sacros*, which means "holy" (the * means that the word is a recreated one). Cognates for this PIE word also include the Latin *sacerdos* "priest" and the Tocharian B word *sakre-* "happy." There may also be a distant connection with the Hittite word saklai- "rite, custom," which is intriguing if you consider that some think "sacred" might also come from the PIE word **sek-* "cut," which, in a ritual sense, could mean to "cut off from the world." So a rite in which something was made sacred could be one where something was set apart from mundane reality. Another interesting word related to the sacred, "consecrate," means to "declare or set apart as sacred," according to the American Heritage College Dictionary. The PIE root for consecrate would have been **weik-*, and this has some interesting cognates as well, such as the Latin *victima* "sacrificial victim" and even the modern word "witch." The Sanskrit cognate, *vinákti*, means to "select out" (Mallory 412). All this suggests that a good definition for the word "sacrifice" might be "to make something set apart from ordinary reality."

So why did the word sacrifice come to have such a negative meaning? The answer may be in the Christian re-making of the word based on the crucifixion of Christ. This sacrifice on the cross summed up all the sacrifices of the Old Testament, and was seen as the last sacrifice ever needed, as it created a new relationship between man and the angry, wrathful God of Judaism (Rogerson 50; Sykes 62, 73-77). So sacrifice came to mean giving up one's life, or, at least, "giving until it hurts." The concept of "giving up" here rather than the ancient religious concept of "giving to" is important and will be covered later in this essay.

Sacrifice as a religious act in Pagan thought appears to have taken place in four ancient contexts as well as in one modern one. They are:

1. Maintaining the Cosmic Order
2. Delivering Services Through Gifts
3. Providing Protection
4. Commensality (Community)
5. Mitigating Order with Chaos (the modern idea)

1. Maintaining the Cosmic Order

There are many myths concerning the creation of the cosmos in the ancient Indo-European (IE) world, but some of them share remarkable similarities. In general, a primordial being is killed or dismembered and from the pieces of his body the universe is made (Lincoln 1986, 2). Sometimes, though not always, the central characters are 'Man' (*Manu*) and 'Twin' (*Yemo*), who is often referred to as a king, and they are sometimes accompanied by an ox. Together they decide to create the universe. The 'Man' would be a priest, and he makes a sacrifice of the other two in order to accomplish their goal. This may be the original PIE creation myth (Lincoln 1991, 7).

In the Rig Veda, the book of hymns from Vedic India, there is a creation myth where Purusha (meaning "Person" according to Mahony, 112) is sacrificed and dismembered by the Gods. It can be found in Book 10, Hymn 90, verses 11-14 (Griffith, 603):

> *When they divided Purusha how many portions*
> *did they make?*
> *What do they call his mouth, his arms?*
> *What do they call his thighs and feet?*
>
> *The Brahman (Priest) was in his mouth,*
> *of both his arms was the Rajanya (Warrior) made.*
> *His thighs became the Vaisya (Commoners),*
> *from his feet the Sudra (Servant) was produced.*[1]

---

[1] This is the only hymn in the Rig Veda that mentions the four castes of Vedic society (Griffith, 603, n.12).

> *The Moon was gendered from his mind,*
> *and from his eye the Sun had birth;*
> *Indra and Agni (Fire) from his mouth were*
> *Born, and Vayu (Wind) from his breath.*
>
> *Forth from his navel came mid-air; the*
> *sky was fashioned from his head;*
> *Earth from his feet, and from his ear the regions .*
> *Thus they formed the worlds.*

In the Poetic Edda, a repository of Norse lore written in Iceland during the 12th or 13th centuries, a similar idea exists. The Lay of Grímnir (*Grímnismál*) has the following stanzas (Hollander, 61):

> *Of Ymir's flesh   the earth was shaped,*
> *of his blood, the briny sea,*
> *of his hair, the trees,   the hills of his bones,*
> *out of his skull the sky.*
>
> *But of his lashes   the loving gods made*
> *Mithgarth for the sons of men;*
> *from his brow they made   the menacing clouds*
> *which in the heavens hover.*

The Romans also had some similar themes in their own lore. It must be remembered that IE mythology in Rome was remembered along civic, rather than religious, lines, where the mythic themes would play out in the 'histories' of the founding of Rome, the monarchical era and even the early Republic (Puhvel, 146-7).

Two myths concerning the founding of the city (the 'cosmos' of Rome) reflect these themes – one of the killing of Twin and the other of dismemberment. In one tale, the twins Romulus and Remus were laying out the walls of the city. Romulus was plowing a furrow to mark the walls while Remus, who had just lost the right to name the new city after himself, taunted his brother by jumping over the furrowed 'wall'. In anger, Romulus killed his brother (Morford, 653-5). The sacred name of

Romulus, Quirinus, (*Co-vir-inos*) comes from the word for 'Man', and the name 'Remus' is cognate (with initial consonantal deformation) to the word **yem-* or 'Twin' (Lincoln, 1984, 174n.3).

Plutarch mentions a story in wide circulation about Romulus in his *Life of Romulus*, chapter 27:

> *But others conjecture that the senators rose up against him and dismembered him in the temple of Hephaistos, distributing his body (among themselves), and each one putting a piece in the folds of his robes in order the carry them away.*

Dionysius of Halicarnassus mentions later that the pieces of his body were buried by the Senators, and Walter Burkert has argued that by being placed in the earth, Romulus *became* the earth, a form of cosmological creation (Lincoln, 1984, 42).

These transformations from the microcosm (Twin) to the macrocosm (creation of cosmos) also occur during sacrifice. IE priests claimed to be doing the same thing, though perhaps on a smaller scale, where each sacrifice would be distributed to the cosmos. Without the matter derived from these offerings, the cosmos and the material world would become exhausted and depleted (Lincoln 1991, 12). Herodotus, in his *History* (1.131) mentions the practices of the Persian priests where sacrifice is given to the cosmos (Rawlingson, 1.131):

> *Their wont, however, is to ascend the summits of the loftiest mountains, and there to offer sacrifice to Jupiter, which is the name they give to the whole circuit of the firmament. They likewise offer to the sun and moon, to the earth, to fire, to water, and to the winds. These are the only gods whose worship has come down to them from ancient times.*

An Indic text, the *Aitareya Brahmana* 2.6, gives instructions as to the handling of the body parts of an animal victim in sacrifice (Lincoln 1991, 13):

> *Lay his feet down to the north. Cause his eye to go to the sun. Send forth his breath to the wind; his*

life-force to the atmosphere, his ears to the cardinal points, his flesh to the earth. Thus the Priest places the victim in these worlds.

But sacrifice is a two-way street. Not only do we offer to sustain the cosmos, but we can also use sacrifice to transfer the power of the universe into our own bodies. Food (through the 'shared meal' taken after sacrifice) and healing are the two prime examples of this. Healing shows up in the story of the healer Dian Cecht and his son, Miach, found in the *Cath Maige Turedh*, (The Second Battle of Moytura) 33-35. The King, Nuadu, cannot rule because he has lost his hand in battle. Dian Cecht makes him a new one of silver, but Miach goes and re-grows the hand on the King's arm, thus infuriating his father. Dian Cecht strikes his son three times, but Miach repairs the damage each time. Finally, the father cuts out his son's brain, and Miach dies. The story continues (Blamires, 115):

After that, Miach was buried by Dian Cecht, and three hundred and sixty-five herbs grew through the grave, corresponding to the number of his joints and sinews. Then Airmed spread her cloak and uprooted those herbs according to their properties. Dian Cecht came to her and mixed the herbs, so that no one knows their proper healing qualities.....

There is a Middle Persian text written after Zarathustra's reforms which tells of the evil spirit Ahriman and his first assault on the 'good creation' in the *Zad Spram* 3.42-51 (Lincoln 1991, 170):

Ahriman came to the cattle. He struggled against the cattle. As the first ox died, because it possessed the nature and form of plants, fifty-seven species of grain and twelve species of healing plants came into being.

Sacrifice is performed to feed the cosmos, as well as the reverse, to regenerate life. The sacrificed animal gives food to the family, promoting life in another form. And as the pruned vines give new and stronger growth so does harvested grain, buried in the ground as seeds, give new grain. It's all a continuing cycle (or circle, if you will) of life and death.

2. Delivering Services Through Gifts

As mentioned earlier, sacrifice is about 'giving to' not 'giving up'. And a good motivation for giving could be the formation of relationships where gifts can be received in return. This idea is well summed up in the Latin phrase, *do ut des*, 'I give so that you may give'.

Ghosti

Yes, it's a strange-looking word, but it is the most fundamental concept in Paganism, and even if you've never seen it before, you are most likely engaging in it in some way.

The term, ***ghos-ti-***, is a recreated Proto-Indo-European root which means, "Someone with whom one has reciprocal duties of hospitality." Cognates include the English words "guest" and "host" as well as the Latin word *hostis*, "enemy," which just shows that strangers could potentially become either friends or enemies (Watkins 31).

Hospitality, and the obligations pertaining to it (on both sides) were extremely important. In the tale of the Trojan War, Zeus resolves to destroy the city because Paris violated the laws of hospitality when he stole Helen away from Sparta while staying as a guest under the hospitality of her husband, Menelaus (Burkert 130).

Relationships based on mutual exchange were similar to "kin" relationships but crossed the boundaries between families and were usually accompanied by ritual gift giving. This would create an obligation of mutual hospitality and friendship that could continue in perpetuity.

One famous example of this type of relationship continuing on through generations is that of Glaucus and Diomedes in the Trojan War. Though on opposite sides of the battle, they discovered that Glaucus' grandfather, Bellerophon, had been a guest of Diomedes' grandfather, Oeneus, years before (Butler, Book VI):

> *"...we two, then, will exchange armour, that all present may know of the old ties that subsist between us."*
>
> *With these words they sprang from their chariots, grasped one another's hands, and plighted friendship.*

Since the time of Hesiod (c. 700 BCE) it was said that the absolute value of a gift to the Gods was not what mattered, but rather that each man should make sacrifice according to his means (Burkert, 274). In other words, those who have more shall give more.

The Greeks carried this to an extreme in their rite called a hecatomb. This rite was a magical act of multiplication. The Greeks would offer one ox in the expectation of receiving 100 oxen from the Gods in return (Burkert 18)!

But the idea of "he who has more shall give more" plays out well in the Patron-Client relationship that appeared in many parts of the Indo-European sphere.

Patron – Client

In this form of reciprocity, called clientship, the patron and client have mutual responsibilities towards each other that form the basis of the relationship. The patron, the richer and more powerful of the two, provides supplies, money or other needs and the client, in return, performs tasks or provides political support. In Rome, the patron might supply a steady income and in return, the client would run errands or vote as he is told.

In ancient Celtic society, clientship was fundamental and a patron's status would depend on the number of clients he had. Since this relationship embraced social, military, political and economic obligations, it was in large part the basis of the power of the nobility. The patron would supply his clients with legal support, political protection, the possibility of sharing in the spoils of war, and even a place filled with the needed tools of farming. In return, the client would pay an annual food rent, supply manual labor, give political support and fight in the patron's army or at least under his command (Green 1995, 92). A patron who was stingy in fulfilling his side of the bargain might not last too long.

In the Irish tale *Cath Maige Turedh* (The Second Battle off Moytura) the Tuatha de Danaan have elevated the half-Formor Bres to the Kingship. However (Blamires, 123),

> *At that time, Bres held the sovereignty as it had been granted to him. There was great murmuring against him among his maternal kinsmen the Tuatha De, for their knives were not greased by him. However frequently they might come, their breaths did not smell of ale; and they did not see their poets nor their bards nor their satirists nor their harpers nor their pipers nor their horn-blowers nor their jugglers nor their fools entertaining them in the household.*

Finally Coirpre son of Etain, the poet of the Tuatha De, pronounces a satire on Bres concerning his stinginess and "there was a blight on him from that hour" (Blamires, 124 & 133). With this blemish Bres could no longer be King.

Another example, this one from Rome, shows clearly the importance of maintaining the reciprocal relationship. There was an ancient, public ritual called the *Evocatio* (evocation) that involved luring the Gods of an enemy city being besieged by the Romans into deserting that city and joining the Roman camp. The Romans would vow to set up a residence and cult for the enemies' Gods among the Romans (Sheid, 104). But part of the ritual involved calling on the Gods to instill fear, terror and *forgetfulness* (italics mine) in the enemy people. Should the enemy forget to make their sacrifices to their Gods, the bonds of reciprocity would be broken. So the Gods, driven forth from the city, would still retain their honor because of the forgetfulness of the people (Lincoln 1991, 232).

The Expectation of Heaven

Heaven in Vedic India was the reward of those who did rigorous penance, or heroes who risk their lives in battle (which resonates with the Norse ideas of Valhalla), but most of all to those who give liberal sacrificial gifts (Macdonell, 167).

In the Rig Veda, Book 1, Hymn 125, verses 1 and 5 (Griffith, 86-87) we see:

Coming at early morn he gives his treasure; the prudent one receives
    and entertains him.
Thereby increasing still his life and offspring, he comes with brave sons to
    abundant riches.

And

On the high ridge of heaven he stands exalted, yea, to the Gods he goes,
    the liberal giver.
The streams, the waters flow for him with fatness : to him this guerdon
    (reward) ever yields abundance.

A Gift Is Part of Oneself

The sacrificer is the person who actually performs the sacrifice, while the sacrifiant is the person who will be receiving the benefit of the sacrifice (Bourdillion, 11). In Vedic culture a householder and his wife would pay the priests to perform a sacrifice, with the intention that the blessings would come to the household. Similarly, in the cities of the Mediterranean, the sacrificers would be professional priests, and the sacrifiants would be the people (or the State). In cases where a person would be performing their own sacrifice, they would be both sacrificer and sacrifiant.

Sacrificers can be priests, sacrificing on behalf of clients or the people, senior members of the family (such as the Roman Paterfamilias) sacrificing for the family, or indeed the supplicant herself. People usually make sacrifices at times of personal or group crisis, or periodically, at special seasonal times, or at the advice of seers or diviners. And what folks usually are doing in sacrifice is performing an act of propitiation, which is done to cause the deities to be favorably inclined, to induce or regain their good will, or to appease or conciliate them (Beattie, 31-32).

In giving, a person gives a part of himself. The best gift a person might give to the Gods would actually be his own life, but a sacrificial offering of oneself is rare. One example might be Decius Mus as recorded by Livy in his *History of Rome*, 10:28. In battle against the Gauls, Decius put on ritual garb and went to the priests (Roberts):

> *After the usual prayers had been recited he uttered the following awful curse: "I carry before me terror and rout and carnage and blood and the wrath of all the gods, those above and those below. I will infect the standards, the armour, the weapons of the enemy with dire and manifold death, the place of my destruction shall also witness that of the Gauls and Samnites." After uttering this imprecation on himself and on the enemy he spurred his horse against that part of the Gaulish line where they were most densely massed and leaping into it was slain by their missiles.*

And thus the battle was won.

The problem with sacrifice of the self is that once you're dead, you can't personally receive any of the benefits of the sacrifice.

Substitution

The ancients came up with a handy solution to this problem through the concept of substitution. In the ancient world, the usual and most ideal substitute for the sacrifiant would be a domestic animal, such as an ox, goat, sheep, etc., to be killed in his stead. Others items were also acceptable, such as precious objects, the first fruits of harvest, etc., but animals were preferred. The reason for the use of domestic animals was that they were identified with the home, the people who lived there and therefore with *man* himself, as opposed to nature or the wild (Beattie, 30-31).

The closest substitutes for the sacrifiant would be another person, a domestic animal, cultivated plants or their products (like wine) and precious objects.

Human Sacrifice

This brings up the question of human sacrifice. The closest substitute for a human being would be another human being. And the choice of the victim would be important. It would need to be someone separate from the community (criminals, strangers, foreigners, slaves) but not too separate, or the substitution might not be of enough equality (Green 2001, 30) to act as a stand-in for the sacrifiants. Often these sacrifices would be for the purpose of averting evil, such as in the Roman 'extraordinary' (Plutarch's word) sacrifice of a pair of Greeks and a pair of Gauls (one male and one female in each couple) in 228 BCE to avert the threat of a Gaulish invasion (Green 2001, 32).

In Acy-Romance in the Ardennes of France, a bizarre burial was found. Over the course of about a century in the 2nd century BCE young men were killed, their bodies placed in a seated position and then desiccated. After drying out, the bodies were buried under the terrace of a temple, accompanied by great feasting on cattle and horses. Each event saw the reburial of a young man in a seated position, either guarding the temple or as a symbol of burial alive. As most other graves were accompanied by cremation and grave goods, this is seen to be a human sacrifice rite, possibly for fertility purposes or as a gift to chthonic gods (Green 2001, 129-130).

As Caesar remarks in his *De Bello Gallico*, 6.16 (Koch, 22):

> *All the people of Gaul are completely devoted to religion, and for this reason those who are greatly affected by diseases and in the dangers of battle either sacrifice human victims or vow to do so using the Druids as administrators to these sacrifices, since it is judged that unless for a man's life a man's life is given back, the will of the immortal gods cannot be placated.*

But human sacrifice was rare in the general course of things, and usually seen as an offering for protection in a time of threat or for the purposes of judicial execution, where a criminal would be "cut off" from society. Indeed, it can be difficult to determine whether the burials found by archeologists are sacrifices or executions or both.

Sacrifice Without Killing

As stated earlier, the killing of animals was a preferred form of sacrifice. Besides the fact that domestic animals made good stand-ins for the sacrifiant, they were also a good form of animal protein for ancient peoples. In fact, in Greece, the only meat that was eaten was sacrificial meat (Green 2001, 42). After all, death is necessary for a carnivorous meal.

But since death is something that is final and irrevocable, it also implies a change of status. A death causes something to no longer be of human use. Once it's gone, it's gone.

So weapons could be 'killed' and offered, and precious objects could be buried or thrown into bodies of water, and therefore go out of human use. The force needed to snap or bend a bronze object would imply violence of a kind, similar to the killing of animals. Weapons, chariot fittings, precious objects and even slave chains have been found in lakes and rivers all over Europe, such as at La Tène in Switzerland, Hayling Island, Hampshire, UK (Green 1995, 470-471) and especially Llyn Cerreg Bach, a lake on Anglessy in Wales, where they even found a trumpet (Green 2001, 183).

Julius Caesar, in *De Bello Gallico* 6.17 (Koch, 22) says of the Gauls and their worship of the God Mars:

> *To him, when they have decided to fight a battle, they consecrate a large part of the plunder;*

Perhaps this is an indication of a warrior cult? In any case, large deposits were made in temples and lakes in the Celtic world. Diodorus Siculus (who wrote between 60-30 BCE) in V.27 states (Koch, 12):

> *The Celts of the interior also have a peculiar custom concerning the sacred places of their gods. In temples and sanctuaries throughout the country, large amounts of gold are openly displayed as dedications to the gods. No one dares to touch these sacred depositions, even though the Celts are an especially covetous people.*

And Strabo (who wrote between 64/63 BCE – CE 21 at least), in his Geography 4.1.13 said (Koch, 15):

> *But as that one [Posidonius] and others have reported, the land, being full of gold and belonging to men who were pious and not extravagant in their living, contained treasures in many places in Celtica. What provided safety more than anything, however, was the lakes into which they had thrown heavy weights of silver and gold.*

Further north in Sweden at the time of the Romans, on Öland and Gotland, deposits of gold rings and various ornaments were found. H.R. Ellis Davidson speculates (131) that these could have been sacrifices to Gods connected to rings, such as Thor, Freyr and Ull, since rings were used in oaths, but that there could have been a fertility connection since the Vanir dispensed wealth and were linked to gold in early skaldic poetry.

Women many have been involved in these sacrifices as well. Danish bog finds at Thorsbjerg included gold rings, personal possessions, pottery and wooden objects and even textiles. Women have a great stake in fertility (Davidson, 132).

First Fruits, Libations, and Votive Offerings

Gregory of Tours in the 6th century CE referred to a lake of the Gabalitani tribe, and stated that in the recent past (Davidson, 132):

> *Into this lake the country people were used to throw, at an appointed time, linen cloths and pieces of material used in male attire, as a firstling sacrifice to this lake. Some threw in woolen fleeces and many also pieces of cheese, wax and thread and various spices, which would take too long to enumerate, each according to his ability. They also used to come with carts, brought with them food and drink, slaughtered animals for the sacrifice and feasted for three days.*

A firstling (or first fruits) sacrifice refers to the idea that the first part of any harvest should be reserved for the Gods. In ancient Greece, whenever a wine jar was opened for drinking, the first cup of wine would be poured on the ground as a libation, again a type of first fruits sacrifice.

Libations were once the most common of sacred acts performed in the ancient world, particularly in the Bronze Age (Burkert, 70). In Greek thought, it stood in opposition to the killing of the animal sacrifice. While the sacrifice burned on the altar, the libation would be poured around it, a sort of ending of hostilities, as it were. Libations poured on the ground were usually intended for the dead or Chthonic Gods under the earth and libations would be made into shafts built into tombs for the dead (for the dead were always thirsty). And it is not only the dead that drink, but the earth as well. Libations were also poured on stones to mark significant spatial orientations, such as at a crossroads (Burkert, 71-73).

A votive offering is an offering made in consequence to a vow. It is usually set up as an 'if – then' formula, such as, "*If,* mighty Gods, my fields produce more grain than last year, *then* I will sacrifice an extra bushel to You!" The vow comes first, and if the desired outcome occurs, then the sacrifice is made. Often, the vows would be to increase first fruit offerings, linking them to the votive offering in a continuing chain of sacrifice.

The types of offerings usually promised in ancient Greece would be simple sacrifices, costly robes or other items, a gift of a slave to a sanctuary, a vow of service to a sanctuary, and even the building of new sanctuaries or shrines, though usually a divine sign would be needed for this (Burkert, 68-70).

3. Apotropaic Offerings for Protection

An apotropaic offering is one having the power to avert an evil influence or bad luck and is a safeguarding against evil. This could be a "Take this sacrifice and go, please!" type offering.

Executions could be considered apotropaic, as they are about removing the criminal from society, to safeguard it from more evil. Even today they take place surrounded by a ritual that prescribes what takes place before the event, the place of witnesses, the manner of killing, etc. (Bourdillon, 13).

Offerings to deities to prevent death and war, or disease, or any other ill would be considered an apotropaic sacrifice. In Greece and Rome, offerings to the dead could be considered apotropaic as well.

Pollution

The removal of dangerous power could only be performed through expiation, which is the act of making amends or reparation for wrong-doing or guilt. In Rome and Greece, this could be done in a variety of ways, including through sacrifice.

A piacular sacrifice (from the Latin *piaculum*) would be any sacrifice offered in expiation for any wrong doing (Scheid, 98), from more minor crimes such as performing a ritual incorrectly all the way up to sacrilege.

In Greece, purification was a social process. To belong to the group led to purity, while to be a reprobate, a rebel or an outsider was to be unclean. So rites of purification were involved with acts of cleaning and in celebrating the removal of filth (physical and spiritual), and the rites elevated people into a higher state, out of a place of genuine discomfort to one of purity (Burkert, 76).

In Rome, purity was connected to piety. Purity was a bodily state not directly related to intentions or morality. Associations with mourning, the dead or dying could lead to an impure state which would require rites of purification ranging from simple ablutions (washing) to periods of waiting. In like manner, washing of hands before a rite would be obligatory. But impiety could encompass more than just purity. The crime of offending a deity could be expiated if the offence were unintentional, but an intentional offence could not be cleansed (Scheid, 26-27).

Purification through water was the chief method in the Greco-Roman world, as it cleaned by removing dirt, but fumigation through censing was also used, as it could remove foul smells and was a primitive form of disinfecting.

In Greece anything that set everyday life out of kilter required purification. This included sexual activity, but other events were far more serious. Contact with death would require extravagant signs of mourning, such as the tearing of hair and clothes, for a certain amount of time, ending with the family purifying themselves by pouring water over their heads, cleaning the house and making a special sacrifice on the hearth. Diseases, especially caused by plagues, were occasions for sacrifice and purification rites, and the purification of a murderer required purification with blood (Burkert, 78-81).

Scapegoat

The word 'scapegoat' actually comes from the Abrahamic Old Testament referring to an actual goat that was used to cleanse the people of sin (Green 2001, 48). But a similar concept existed in the Indo-European world as well.

In Greece, the *pharmakos* is a man chosen on account of his ugliness and is feasted on figs, barley broth and cheese, and then he is whipped out with fig branches and sea onions, and very importantly, he is struck seven times on his penis (Burkert, 82). The idea is that an animal or person is used to carry the pollution of the city or group away, which purifies everyone else.

One thing that appears necessary is for the scapegoat to be first brought into intimate contact with the community or city, so that he can absorb, as it were, the pollution there. After he is driven out, only purity remains (Burkert, 83).

Oxen and beautiful maidens could also be scapegoats (Burkert, 84) though men were more likely. And in Greece, the scapegoat might not be killed necessarily (Green 2001, 145), and adolescents chosen for this role might even have gone through rites to reincorporate them back into the community.

One famous example of the death of the scapegoat is from the Greek city of Massilia in southern Gaul. There, a poor citizen volunteered himself on behalf of the town. For a year the people of Massalia feted and cosseted him, and then at the end of the year they dressed him up in a sacred robe and leaf crown, led him through the city with the people cursing him all the way, and then murdered him (Green 2001, 145).

Hellenic Oath Sacrifice

The Hellenic oath sacrifice could be seen as the reverse of an apotropaic rite, in that terror and destruction are used to bind an oath, giving it the greatest importance. Here, after sacrifice, the oath-maker plunges his hands into a bucket of the animal's blood and then treads on the severed genitals of the animal, compounding bloodshed with castration. And acts of self-cursing follow to really bind the act, asking utter destruction to fall upon the oath-breaker and his line – with killing off the family corresponding to castration (Burkert, 251).

4. Commensality – The Shared Meal

A common part of the sacrificial process in the ancient world was the cooking and eating of the flesh of the sacrificial animal. In Greece, only meat obtained through sacrifice could be eaten (Green 2001, 42) – they didn't have butchers on the street corners. These sacrificial rites were the occasion of great feasting and joy. The sharing of food symbolized and enhanced the unity of the people in celebration. It also allowed for communion with the Gods invoked (Bourdillion, 20).

Generally, in Greece, only the skin, bones and fat were given to the Gods while the rest was reserved for the people. Feasting was extremely important at any festival, and continues to be so today.

And in the patron-client relationship, the client provides food rent to the Patron in return for protection, a share in the spoils, etc. The sharing of food with the Gods in the shared meal also reflects this human bargain, giving man the right to make demands upon the Gods.

5. Chaos Mitigating Cosmos (Modern)

Finally, we come to the modern form of sacrifice that appears in current practice. If cosmos equals order, and chaos equals lack of order, then there is an area in between the two, a sort of liminal place where order and chaos are in balance. While too much chaos causes everything to fall apart, too much order can cause brittleness. Ceisiwr Serith introduced the idea that chaos can feed cosmos in 2000 (Serith).

Imagine a pine tree in a hurricane. The tree's lack of flexibility will cause the tree to snap in the storm. But a supple palm tree will bend with the wind, its leaves folding back to protect the heart from the wind, and after the storm has passed, the palm tree will usually spring back as if nothing had happened.

In parts of the ancient world, rituals had to be performed absolutely correctly or the Gods would be offended. In Rome, if there were some error or omission committed in a rite, the pontiffs would first have to perform a rite of expiation (*piaculum*) to conciliate the offended God, and then repeat the badly performed rite all over again (Scheid, 117). Spontaneity was frowned upon.

In modern times, however, some spontaneity is valued because too much predictability and order can be seen as boring. Spontaneous prayers and offerings of praise can be seen as positive additions to any rite. Here, the mitigation of cosmos (order) with a bit of chaos (disorder) can be a good thing. No matter how carefully organized a Praise Offering section of a modern rite may be, there is always the element of uncertainty involved when the people have their chance to praise, sing, dance or do whatever it is that they have elected to do as a sacrifice for the Gods. This bit of chaos mitigates the normal order of any rite, giving it life.

Sacrifice For Modern Pagans

Let's face it, the killing of animals just isn't acceptable for most people in public ritual, and the killing of people is guaranteed to get one into a great deal of trouble.

But we need to have something to give to the Kindreds so that they might give back to us in return, and here substitution comes to the rescue. Items made by the sacrifiants or valuables owned by them make wonderful sacrifices, to be thrown in the Well (for later disposal) or hung on the Tree.

Food and drink was often given to the Powers in the ancient world, and we can do the same today. Items the ancients used include oil and butter (or ghee) offered to the Fire, wine to the fire altar (but remember that wine and beer don't burn and will put your fire out if poured directly on the flames), and other foodstuffs can be offered to the Fire, etc., as well. Remember that non-flammable libations are best when poured directly on the ground.

Weapons like swords can be 'killed' by breaking or bending them, or they can just be offered whole to the Well or a shaft or buried in the ground. Likewise hand-made items can be broken or buried or otherwise given to the Kindreds.

Apotropaic offerings are already being performed in ADF in the form of the Outdwellers offering that many of us do. This bribe would be a propitiatory offering. We also perform purifications through the use of water and incense or sage (Water and Fire). Rites and sacrifices of expiation can also be performed for failed oaths and for squabbles among the People. Anytime we fail to live up to our promises, it may be best to get right with the Gods.

Another idea would be to make a doll and give it a place of honor in your rites. At the end of a specified time (a month or a year, say), it can be reviled and burned in the fire as a scapegoat, carrying with it any discord or disharmony in the Grove and the lives of the People. Even a Wicker Man could be used for this purpose, to 'burn away' any impurity felt by the Grove or solitary, or to carry hand-written 'messages' from the People to the Gods.

We already perform Praise Offerings in many Groves, and any poems, songs, chants or dances created by a sacrifiant would be an excellent sacrifice to the Kindreds, mitigating cosmos with a bit of chaos.

And finally, the Shared Meal is a wonderful way of joining with each other and the Kindreds in an act of unity. Part of a loaf of bread or other food could be offered to the Spirits, and the rest eaten by the People. And in Groves that have potlucks, a portion of each dish could be given to the Kindreds through the Fire or to the Land before the People eat.

So, What Does All This Mean?

Sacrifice was an integral part of religion, worship and spirituality in the ancient world, without which there would have been no public religion. The concept of reciprocity enables us to give and to receive the blessings we require for our hearts and spirits, giving us a roadmap for our physical as well as our spiritual lives. And even though we aren't those ancient peoples, these simple ideas can work for us today, bringing us closer to the Gods and other Spirits, that we might know Them, and They, us.

Praying With a Good Fire

What does it mean to "pray with a good fire?"

The phrase "may we pray with a good fire" is an old and truly Indo-European phrase, conjuring images of not only a fire of piety within us, where we ignite that religious or spiritual fire, but also of the physical fire before us, to which we make offerings.

All fires are sacred, and our religion, if it could truly be defined beyond "earth-based religion," might best be called a "fire religion" because of the central focus that fire serves for our rituals.

By "praying with a good fire," we recognize both the fire within and the fire without, the piety of both our belief and our actions: we do not come before our gods empty-handed.

Further Reading on This Chapter's Concepts

Beattie, J.H.M. 'On Understanding Sacrifice' in Bourdillon, M.F.C. and Meyer Fortes, Editors 1980. *Sacrifice*. New York: Academic Press, Inc., pp. 29-44.

Blamires, Steve 1995. *The Irish Celtic Magical Tradition: Ancient Wisdom of the Battle of Moytura*. London, San Francisco: Thorsons (HarperCollins).

Bourdillon, M.F.C. and Meyer Fortes, Editors 1980. *Sacrifice*. New York: Academic Press, Inc.

Burkert, Walter. John Raffin, Translator 1985. *Greek Religion*. Cambridge, MA: Harvard University Press.

Butler, Samuel, translator. Homer, "The Illiad". (March 20, 2008). http://classics.mit.edu//Homer/iliad.html

Davidson, H.R. Ellis 1988. *Myths and Symbols in Pagan Europe: Early Scandinavian and Celtic Religions*. Syracuse, NY: Syracuse University Press.

Green, Miranda, Editor 1995. *The Celtic World*. London and New York: Routledge.

Green, Miranda Aldhouse 2001, *Dying for the Gods*. Charleston, SC: Tempus Publishing Inc.

Griffith, Ralph T.H., Translator 1992. *Sacred Writings: Hinduism – The Rig Veda*. New York: Book-Of-The-Month-Club (Motilal Banarsidass Publishers)

Hollander, Lee M., Translator, 1962. *The Poetic Edda*. Austin, Texas: University of Texas Press.

Koch, John T. and John Carey, Editors 2000. *The Celtic Heroic Age: Literary Sources for Ancient Celtic Europe & Early Ireland & Wales*. Oakville and Aberystwyth: Celtic Studies Publications.

Lincoln, Bruce 1986. *Myth, Cosmos, and Society: Indo-European Themes of Creation and Destruction*. Cambridge: Harvard University Press.

Lincoln, Bruce 1991. *Death, War, and Sacrifice: Studies in Ideology and Practice*. Chicago: University of Chicago Press.

Macdonell, A.A. 2002. *Vedic Mythology*. Delhi: Motilal Banarsidass Publishers Private Ltd.

Mahony, William K. 1998. *The Artful Universe: An Introduction to the Vedic Religious Imagination*. Albany, NY: State University of New York Press.

Mallory, J.P. and D.Q. Adams 2006. *The Oxford Introduction to Proto-Indo-European and the Proto-Indo-European World*. Oxford: Oxford University Press.

Morford, Mark P.O. and Robert J. Lenardon, 2003. *Classical Mythology*, Seventh Edition. New York and Oxford: Oxford University Press.

Puhvel, Jaan, 1987. *Comparative Mythology*. Baltimore and London: The Johns Hopkins University Press.

Rogerson, J.W. 'Sacrifice in the Old Testament' in Bourdillon, M.F.C. and Meyer Fortes, Editors 1980. *Sacrifice*. New York: Academic Press, Inc., pp. 45-59.

Rawlingson, George, translator. Herodotus, "The History of Herodotus" (March 20, 2008), http://classics.mit.edu/Herodotus/history.1.i.html

Roberts, Rev. Canon, translator. Titus Livius, *The History of Rome, Vol. II'* (March 20, 2008), http://etext.lib.virginia.edu/toc/modeng/public/Liv2His.html

Serith, Ceisiwr, 2000. 'Sacrifice, The Indo-Europeans, and ADF' (March 28, 2008), http://www.adf.org/articles/cosmology/sacrifice-ie-adf.html

Sheid, John 2003. *An Introduction to Roman Religion*. Bloomington and Indianapolis: Indiana University Press.

Sykes, S.W. 'New Testament and Christian Theology' in Bourdillon, M.F.C. and Meyer Fortes, Editors 1980. *Sacrifice*. New York: Academic Press, Inc., pp. 61-83.

Watkins, Calvert, Editor 2000. *The American Heritage Dictionary* of Indo-European Roots. Boston: Houghton Mifflin Co.

Personal Ritual Work

With all those mechanical things out of the way, let's dive in a bit to the basics of doing personal ritual work: purification, the home shrine, and prayer.

Learning to Cleanse and Purify

Before coming before our Ancestors, our Allies among the Spirits of Nature, or the Shining Gods and Goddesses, we do well to purify ourselves in some way.

This is not to suggest that the physical body is somehow base or something to be ashamed of; rather, you could liken the process of purification and cleansing to washing your hands after you visit the restroom: it is only polite to wash away those things that others may prefer not to come into contact with.

Every day, we come into contact with things that leave us a bit dirty: worry, stress, and anger are some of those things. Leaving them behind is an important step in the process of preparing ourselves to greet the Kindreds at the Center of Worlds. How you work this purification is up to you, but here are some suggestions.

Purification by Fire and Water

This is probably the most common form of purification in Neopaganism: it involves washing or sprinkling yourself with holy water and allowing the smoke from a fire or incense to wash over you. Just as purification with water is akin to washing your hands, purification through fire is the ancient equivalent of putting on deodorant: it is only polite to approach the gods smelling nice.

If you feel the need to purify your space, you can also use fire and water to do this. Walk around your space and chant the following:

> *By the Might of the Waters, and the Light of the Fire,*
> *This Grove is made Whole and Holy!*

Purification by Hand-Washing

A very ancient form of purification, hand-washing is an excellent way to re-purify yourself during a ritual if you feel you need it (for instance, you had to run out of the ritual space to retrieve an item you forgot to bring inside). It can also be done when first entering the space.

Leave a bowl with water and a clean hand-towel next to your ritual area, and as you enter it (or leave it on your altar for use in ritual) dip your hands in the water, pour water over each hand with the other, and rub your hands together briefly before drying them on the cloth. Chant the following:

> *These Waters were won by the gods for me:*
> *As they run over my hands and return to themselves,*
> *Let them wash away all negative things.*

Purification by Focus

Similar to how the hand-washing can purify you using only water and not fire, you can also purify yourself with fire. If you carry around a set of matches and a tealight (these two items fit beautifully in most mint tins), you will carry your fire wherever you go, and any fire that is kindled with intent is also a good fire, and the hands that kindle such a fire are blessed by the warmth of that fire.

Speak the following as you kindle the flame:

> *The Fire shines bright!*
> *The Fire burns hot!*
> *The darkness is banished!*
> *Let me pray with a good fire!*

Purification by Bathing

This is the single most common recommended form of purification in Neopagan literature, but it's also the least likely to be useful; after all, when was the last time you really felt like you needed to pray *and* you had time for a bath?

Still, if you have both the time and the ability to take a bath before your working, you are likely to find many benefits to doing so, particularly if you also use the bath in conjunction with one of the other methods listed here.

Full Body Bath:
The waters flow from the earth,
And I descend as the sun into them.
Where they are, I am brightened.
Where they are, I am cleansed.

Partial Bath:
Cleansed with the Shining Waters,
My hands are quietly blessed.
Armored by the Shining Waters,
My heart is given depth of strength.
Purified by Shining Waters,
My will is given wings to fly.

Shower:
I greet the Waters as they flow over me,
Running down my face,
Running down my back,
Running down my legs.
The Waters make me shine,
And purify me for the work ahead.

Building a Shrine

One of the most important works you can do as a Pagan is to build and honor the deities at a shrine.

Altars, Shrines and Tables

Altars, shrines, and tables are entirely separate things, but we tend to use the terms fairly interchangeably in modern Neopaganism. It is worth noting the difference between each type of ritual surface, because many will find the terms shed new light on the manner in which they will work.

An **Altar** is, most properly, the structure upon which the fire is kindled for sacrifice. Since Christianity's dominance, most people do not expect to find fires on their altars, but this is their original purpose. The process of building an altar was carefully described in many ancient religions, and was of the utmost importance, because every fire that is kindled is a deity, and you are building that deity's seat when you build the altar.

For the most intense and memorable example of the painstaking process that altar-building can be, look no further than the agnicyana ritual, where the fire altar is built of 395 bricks in five layers, in the shape of a falcon. Most Vedic fire altars were probably made of 21 bricks.

Also, "altar" is spelled with an "-ar" at the end, not an "-er."

A **Shrine** is a place where deity images, statues, or other such objects are kept and venerated. While there may be a place to set or deposit offerings, the shrine rarely has its own "working space" where one would work magic or extensive religious ritual. The word itself comes from precursors meaning "box" or "case." Some shrines are portable and some are permanent; all of them, though, create deep connections with the Spirits.

An ideal example of these are the Greek *kandylakia*, or roadside shrines, that you come across throughout the Greek countryside. These are small shrines that most often contain a votive candle and an image of a saint who either helped the person escape a close call with death, or the saint that the family prays will take care of an individual who died during a crash. In modern America, you can see shrines in the form of religious markers next to the road where accidents have killed individuals.

The main purpose of a shrine is veneration and prayer, and it will become part of your daily spiritual life. Each day, you should expect to encounter the Holy at your shrine, however you define it.

A **Table** is the traditional workspace that we think of when we think on spellwork, ritual work, or "the place I put my tools when I'm not using them just now." All those "altar" diagrams encountered in those books on "how to be a witch" or "how to do Celtic Magick" are actually diagrams of tables.

You likely should have a table in your ritual space so that you can work comfortably and lay things out: in fact, you probably should have such a thing. Just remember what it is, and call it by its correct name.

Building the Shrine

Most people will begin with a shrine (altars are hard to do when you don't have access to an outdoor place to burn things, and tables seem superfluous to someone who doesn't have a shrine). Start with these simple steps:

1. **Clear a spot** that you can dedicate just to honoring the Spirits – This should not be someplace you will put the mail, put your keys, or place things that will "clutter" the space.
2. **Place a candle** or incense burner in that space – This is the simplest form of devotion.
3. **Place a vessel** of water in the space – You can use this to purify, to sink offerings of silver, or to represent the waters that balance the fire.
4. **Find a deity image** or something that reminds you of the divine – This does not need to be complicated or fancy, just something that speaks to you.
5. **Light the candle and pray.** And that's it!

Writing Simple Prayers

One of the first steps, once you have your shrine space, is to begin to approach the beings that move your heart. These beings may or may not be known to you, but you can always begin by writing a simple prayer, lighting a candle, and speaking that prayer to the cosmos.

Types of Prayer

1. **Adoratory:** Prayers of Praise – These are prayers that sing about the great things that a deity or spirit has done for you, for others, or in general. Think about the mythology of the being, and try to apply that to the prayer in some way. Remember, this is about praise, not thanks (see the next category).
2. **Thanksgiving:** Prayers of Thanks – When the Spirits have done something great for you, it is proper to send a "Thank You" note. Since the deities have little use for

paper cards, the best thing is to offer them a prayer that tells them what you thought about their gift.

3. **Petitionary:** Prayers of Request – The reciprocity of exchange and gifting that Paganism is founded on means that we can occasionally ask for things. Often, we provide reminders about why we're eligible for these things (our deities, remember, are limited), and tell them why we're asking for them.

4. **Expiatory:** Prayers of Apology – Sometimes, we do something that is "wrong." We break our word, fail to follow through, and sometimes just do stupid things. Prayers of expiation make these things right again by re-making the cosmos for us.

5. **Loving:** Prayers of Love – These are very similar to adoratory prayers, but have a key difference: this is less about "you're so great" and more about "I love you because…" Think about it as the difference between praising a co-worker and telling your spouse about how much you love him or her.

6. **Meditation:** Prayers of Focus – These prayers are all about asking for focus. Most commonly, these are prayers that draw us deeper into ourselves, or prayers that lift our souls to the heavens. Mantras, litanies, and highly internalized and memorized prayers are the most common meditative prayers.

Or, to put it simply, prayers tend to make the following general statements:

Hallelujah, Thanks, Please, Sorry, I Love You, and "____"

Each of these prayers can also be formulated along a general outline, and knowing that outline can help you when you are at a loss for words and really just want to (or need to!) pray.

Each one starts with the most important thing (knowing who to pray to and your reason for that prayer) and ends with the second most important thing (thanking them). It's the center of the prayer sandwich that changes.

Adoratory (Praise) Prayers: A Formula

0. Know who you are praying to, and a reason to praise them
1. "Address" the prayer
2. Tell the addressee how awesome they are
   a. Draw on myth
   b. Draw on personal experience
   c. Draw on community experience
3. Thank them for listening

Thanksgiving Prayers: A Formula

0. Know who you are praying to
1. "Address" the prayer
2. Explain those things that you are thankful for
3. Say something about how you are thankful for them
   a. Begin each thing with, "We are thankful for"
   b. End each thing with, "For this, we are thankful."
   c. Provide a general, "You have given us many things, including" to start the list
4. Thank them once more for all the things listed
   a. "For all these things and more, we thank you."
   b. "We give X in thankfulness for all these things." (with optional offering)

Petitionary/Supplication Prayers: A Formula

0. Know what you are praying about
1. Start by "addressing" the prayer
2. Tell the addressee how awesome they are
3. Tell them who you are
4. Tell/Remind them:
   a. Why you should be important to them

       b. Of things you have done together in the past
5. Ask for what you want or need
       a. Reflect the being's awesomeness
6. Say what you will do in return
7. Thank the being

Expiatory Prayers: A Formula

0. Know what you did wrong, and who you must address expiation to
1. "Address" your prayer to the appropriate beings
2. Remind the addressee of why they are interested in your prayer
       a. Indicate the time, date, or other information about when the bargain was struck or the oath taken
       b. Describe the terms (what was promised or received)
3. Explain what you did not do
       a. Indicate any oaths/bargains made that are not fulfilled
       b. Indicate any portions of oaths/bargains that are unfulilled
       c. Include any item or events that prevented fulfillment
4. Explain what you will do in recompense
5. Thank the addressee for their understanding

Loving Prayers: A Formula

0. Know who you wish to address your love to
1. "Address" your prayer
2. Tell the being how much you love them
3. Thank the addressee for listening

Meditative Prayers: An Exception

There really is no formula for meditative prayers. Often, these are short mantras (phrases chanted over and over) or litanies ("call and response" prayers that have a single line that is repeated between lines that change). One good example of a mantra might be:

"Indra, Strike Me Not!"

Repeating that prayer over and over during a thunderstorm can help you focus and drive away a fear of thunderstorms.

Three Things For Every Invocation/Evocation/Invitation/Calling

While certainly not every prayer or ritual piece is the same, there are some things that you can remember that will help you out in all ritual situations.

1. **Have three points to make** – Often, making a single point or covering a single aspect of a deity seems like more can be said, and two points or two aspects will often leave you feeling as if your prayer is unfinished. Three points will provide balance and will help you feel like your prayer is complete. Compare, "O Taranis, who draws the clouds together," to "O Taranis, who brings the rains, drawing the clouds together, and feeding the earth!"

2. **Don't sweat the repetition** – In prayer, like poetry, it is considered a skill to say the same thing in different ways. Repetition of a key point (or even a key phrase) can go a long way toward making your point stick in your mind. In a prayer to the fire (the Vedic god's name is Agni), you might say: "O Agni, your flames reach toward the heavens, your tongue devours the ghee as you grow in strength, and your face brightens the home!" These three statements say the same thing (the fire is getting brighter), but they say it differently.

3. **Memorize "bookends"** – If you start strong and end strong, the "middle" of the prayer will sound better to you (and anyone listening) on reflection. It is good if you have something to begin each prayer (e.g. "I call to ____, who I have called to before!"), and good if you have something to end each prayer (e.g. "So join me, ____. Come to my fire and receive my offerings. You are welcome here.").

If you plan three points, get comfortable with repetition, and memorize just one opening statement and one closing statement, you will find that it is much easier to speak to the Powers in your own voice.

Exercise: Writing A Prayer

It is time to get to work: write a prayer! Select the type you want to write, and then get to it! For this exercise, make it about 6-10 lines long.

Developing Personal Rituals

From the immediate intimacy of solitary prayer, we move to a more robust form of worship: solitary ritual.

Making the Commitment

"Practice does not make perfect; only perfect practice makes perfect."
– Vince Lombardi

Everything starts with building good ritual habits: the primary purpose of this book is really to help you develop and build those practices over time. The practices, though, all begin with one thing: making the commitment to do the work. Once you have done that, you just need to start following through. One step at a time, though!

Start with these six simple things, and follow through on them with every rite that you do, and you will find very quickly that you have become far more comfortable than you thought you would be.

1. **When doing ritual alone, do ritual as if in public:** after all, when you invite the Kindreds in, you are never truly alone. Think of yourself as having an "audience" that you are preforming in front of, and be conscious of the attention that the Kindreds pay to you. It may make you more comfortable to remember that modern Paganism is only about 100 years old at best, so we're all just learning: even the best public priest you've seen had awkward moments at her personal altar when she started!

2. **Speak out loud, not just in your head!** If you never speak out loud at your own altar, you will never find a way to speak with a sure, certain voice when you are in public. You will also find that speaking aloud brings a certain discipline to your practice: you cannot skip through things quickly, and all things become more and more deliberate.

3. **Practice movement and gestures.** The body is connected to our religious experiences in ways that might surprise you: having consistent, planned actions that we physically do (even if they are as simple as sitting in the same way, or folding your hands across your lap at the same point in a particular prayer) will enhance the experience in amazing ways.

4. **Make physical offerings.** It is too easy to let ourselves "off the hook" for physical offerings when we are alone, but part of the reason that we make physical offerings is to remind us (and the Kindreds) that we, as Pagans, consider the physical world just as sacred as the non-physical. To abandon physical offerings is the first step to denying the physical, something we should never do.

5. **Practice at the same time each day, and make commitments of 15 days or more.** It is said it takes 15 days to create a good habit: when you think about starting a new practice, or trying something again, make a personal commitment to both the time of day and the length of time you'll do it for.

6. **Keep a journal** (particularly of your omens!). You will often want to return to this journal (and you should do it regularly even if you don't want to, perhaps on the first of the month) to review where you have been on your path. One of the crazy things about omens is that they often make better sense once some time has passed.

Deepening connections

As you continue to work and do daily devotionals you will notice that your relationships with the Kindreds change. This is a normal part of developing a relationship; just like when you meet new people and build a friendship. As we discussed earlier, the **ghosti-* relationship is one of mutual exchange and obligations. You will begin to have a rapport with your Kindreds and based on lore and that rapport you will begin to develop Unverified Personal Gnosis (**UPG**) that will deepen your understanding of and connection to the Kindreds.

The other thing that happens when doing daily rituals or devotions is the repetition helps you find your voice and allows to craft your liturgy. Much like a musician learning the scales on the piano, the dancer practicing the same routine or the wide receiver of a football team running routes by doing things over and over you are building a mental discipline and an "event" or "muscle" memory that will become part of your spiritual vocabulary.

Think of it like this: every musician has a bag of tricks that they develop over time. For a guitarist the endless, boring practice of scales and chords day after day does more than build blisters on her fingers they help her to begin to hear what notes belong together and help her motor skills and hands begin to build a bridge to her subconscious and later when she needs the information she will have not only recall but a feel for what works. Creating prayers, chants and devotionals are the same way. It is by creating a system that works for you and then allowing inspiration take over. The basic scales you learn playing piano or guitar are just spring boards to the melody and magic that will come later.

The deepening continues when you begin working with a group. By sharing common liturgy, cosmology and theology then the core ritual team grows tighter and stronger. It is from this core team that you can take the lessons learned in your hearth practice and transform them into dynamic public rituals.

Ritual Outlines

Going from "prayer" to "ritual" is not as hard as you might think: generally speaking, it can be done quickly and easily, once you realize that most ritual outlines are really just roadmaps with big, blinking lights that say, "Put Prayer Here!" There are a few places where it gets a bit complicated, but these are few and far between.

Having an outline that covers what you do "every time" is a good idea. It allows you to be less dependent on scripts, and provides a consistent structure that will help you remember what comes next. Just as you have "bookends" for prayers, your common Order of Ritual will help you remember where you are and where you're going.

Here are three basic ritual outlines that should help you work through the transition from prayer to rite.

The ADF Core Order of Ritual

1. Initiating the Rite – May include:
   - Musical Signal
   - Opening Prayer
   - Processional
   - Establishing the Group Mind
2. Purification - This must take place prior to Opening the Gates
3. Honoring the Earth Mother
4. Statement of Purpose
5. (Re)Creating the Cosmos
   - Sacred Center must be established in a triadic Cosmos
   - The Three Worlds or Realms must be acknowledged
   - The Fire must be included
   - Sacred Center is most commonly represented as Fire, Well and Tree
6. Opening the Gate(s) - Must include a Gatekeeper
7. Inviting the Three Kindreds
8. Key Offerings - This will commonly include:
   - Invitation of Beings of the Occasion
   - Seasonal customs as appropriate
   - Praise Offerings
9. Prayer of Sacrifice
10. Omen
11. Calling (asking) for the Blessings
12. Hallowing the Blessing
13. Affirmation of the Blessing
14. Workings (if any)
15. Thanking the Beings
16. Closing the Gate(s)
17. Thanking the Earth Mother
18. Closing the Rite

Three Cranes Grove, ADF, Druid Moon Order

1. (Re)Creating the Cosmos/Attunement of the Folk to Each Other
2. Opening the Sacred Center
3. Gatekeeper Offerings and Gate Opening
4. Processional and Challenge
5. Attunement to Space
6. Honoring the Earth
7. Other opening prayers
8. Honoring the Kindreds/Beings of the Occasion
9. Praise
10. Prayer of Sacrifice
11. Omens
12. Magical Work
13. Thanking
14. Recessional/Hugs
15. Thanking the Gatekeeper
16. Closing the Gates
17. Dismantling the Space/More Hugs

General Pagan Order

1. Purify
2. Cast a Circle
3. Call quarters/directions
4. Honor the deities
5. Magical Work
6. Thank the deities
7. Thank the quarters/directions
8. Open the Circle
9. Ground & Center

Using an Outline

Outlines are best used to help you break down a rite into smaller chunks, and to find your place when you forget what comes next (even people with a lot of experience forget where they're going in a ritual from time to time).

You can start by writing a prayer for each basic section, and determining if you want to provide an offering as well. Some items, like "casting a circle" or "magical work," are not well defined in this book, but the suggested reading at the end does provide a number of sources that will help in these sections.

Always start with an outline: it will make the process of creating your rite dramatically easier.

Center and Circumference

"The Center is everywhere, the circumference nowhere."
-Joseph Campbell

"Remember, no matter where you go, there you are."
-Buckaroo Banzai

There is a Zuni legend that when the Water Skate was given magical powers by the Sun Father, he stretched his four legs out upon the waters.

His front right leg stretched first to the northeast, the place of the summer solstice sunrise; his front left leg stretched next to the northwest, the place of the summer solstice sunset; his back left leg then stretched to the southwest, the place of the winter solstice sunset; his back right leg then stretched to the southeast, the place of the winter solstice sunrise.

Where his heart then rested marked the "Center Place," the center of the land that is surrounded by the four seas and the heart of the Earth Mother. It is below this center, below the heart of the Water Skate which is the heart of the Earth Mother, that the village of Zuni was established.

At the center of the village, another center resides. This is on a permanent altar in the chief priest's house, where a heart-shaped rock (known as "the heart of the world") rests. Within this rock are arteries that reach toward the four solstice points.

These centers, it is easy to see, form a series of centers that are both atop each other in an obvious layering effect and also all the same in their overlay. None of these centers can exist without the others, and they seem to form around one another in ever tightening rings. Each center is itself, unique; each center is also all the other centers.

Eliade indicates that religion itself is an orienting force, one that gives us a focal point from which to make sense of the world. When we are in a profane state, one that is not sacred, we have no point of reference. It is only through the breakthrough of the sacred into the profane world, the hierophany, that orientation is possible. "The heirophany reveals an absolute fixed point, a center."

It is the finding of this fixed point, this center, which allows us to make sense of the world. If religion is indeed about finding ways to orient ourselves, to place ourselves in relative location to everything else, then we must find those centers, even if we must create them. The creation of those centers is similar to founding the cosmos.

Centers themselves are different from the rest of the world. They are places that allow this orientation, an orientation that the profane world cannot provide. Many of us are familiar with the *axis mundi*, or the axis of the world from Eliade. These cosmic pillars can only exist, according to Eliade, at the center of the universe, and all things extend about it. It supports the sky and finds its roots deep within the earth, and its presence is not an ordering force, but a break, a rip in the fabric of the profane world that allows the sacred to pour into and destroy the homogeneity of space.[2]

The destruction of the homogenous space is made possible by openings to other worlds, allowing travel and communication between them. In the case of the Zuni, there are four upper worlds and four underworlds that the *axis mundi* allows access to. Time also begins at the center, and mythical time exists at the outskirts of their cosmos.[3]

In Druidic cosmology, we find that the center of the world has three parts: Well, Fire, and Sacred Tree. Often, we think of the Tree as the *axis mundi*, but it is not the only center in ritual. Indeed, all the hallows are a center, and they combine to form the center. The center is not complete with only the tree, for while the tree grows high and is rooted deep, it cannot devour our sacrifices as the fire can, nor can it carry our voices to the depths of the earth as the well can.

Instead, the center must make use of all parts of the hallows: Well, Fire, and Tree. Beyond that, though, there is also

---

[2] For further reading on Eliade's theory of hierophany and centers, see "The Sacred & the Profane: The Nature of Religion" by Mircae Eliade. ISBN: 015679201X

[3] For the Water Skate myth and Zuni centers, see "New Directions in American Archeoastronomy", edited by Anthony F. Aveni: Oxford, England: 1988. ISBN 0860545830. The article in question is "Directionality as a Conceptual Model for Zuni Expressive Behavior" by M. Jane Young.

the center of the earth, the heart of the Earth Mother, upon whose breast we build our Fire, root our Tree, and sink our Well. We establish the center above her heart, above the center of the earth.

The Grove itself has a center, the place in the middle of those Grove members gathered that the energies and the focus of the ritual are centered. Within each other, we find our own orientation, our own center: there is no stronger center, no larger axis, no more powerful hierophany than that of a Grove standing together, orienting themselves to one another, and finding their place in the centers others can offer.

Most important, though, is another center that must not only be found, but that the ritual cannot happen without: the center of ourselves. Each of us, within our own heart, must find the center of our beings, the inner center that allows us to stand in the center, to be our own *axis mundi*. From us, all things radiate, and within ourselves we can discover a rift between the sacred and the profane.

If we cannot find the center of ourselves, if the hierophany of our hearts cannot be seen, then others cannot find it within us. If the Grove cannot orient itself by combining these centers, then it cannot find the center of the earth, the heartbeat of the Earth Mother. If we cannot orient ourselves to that center, then we cannot orient our hallows, and the Well, Fire, and Tree will not stand at the center of the worlds.

Centers are unlike any other thing in ritual: they are where we establish them. Yes, they can appear naturally, and there are places that a center is more likely to appear than others, but to truly do the work of magic, we need to learn to establish them, to place them atop one another, to blend them and to maintain their distinctions. We must find them in ourselves, either through meditation or ritual, and we must learn to use the point of reference created by our own center to orient ourselves to the other centers around us.

As Joseph Campbell said, "The center is everywhere; the circumference is nowhere."

Ways to Find Your Center

"At our center burns a Living Flame."
-Ceisiwr Serith

Each of us has a center that we call "home," though not all of us know where that center is within us. Here are a few ways to find that center and learn where it is for future work.

- Light a candle and pray for a moment. Feel around in your body for where that "center" might be. Don't "hunt and peck," but just take note of how your body feels and where you feel most "centered" or "heavy."
- Focus on your breathing. After you have focused on a few in-breaths and out-breaths, try to focus on where the air is going. Listen to see if you can hear your heartbeat. Can you follow these sounds to your center?
- Choose a point inside your body to be your center, such as:
  - Behind your forehead (pineal gland)
  - Your heart
  - Your stomach
  - Your groin (root chakra)

Crossing the Boundaries, Painting the Cosmos

Much of what we do in ritual is designed, not to climb from the material world into the perfected spiritual world, for such a directional movement inherently denies the value of this world, but to seek to manifest the spiritual in this realm. The path of modern Paganism in general prefers to seek to perfect and purify the physical world through ritual and the participation in the ways of the Cosmos, what the Vedics called *Rta*, the Indo-Iranians called *asha*, the Norse called *orlog*, and the Proto-Indo-Europeans might have called **artus*.

This is why we do not leave this world when we do ritual. While Abrahamic traditions seek to transcend this world, Hindus seek an inner world, and Buddhists seek to escape the suffering of the world, modern Paganism instead seeks to work *in* this world *for* this world.

Internal Gates and External Gates

There is a concept within ADF of ritual "Gates" that are opened in ritual. We don't open the Gates because the Spirits can't hear us, or because we are separated from them in our daily lives. We open the Gates in order to ease communication by centering ourselves within the worlds.

We can describe the process of "Opening the Gates" in fairly simple terms, even though it's a fairly complex magical action. ADF takes a fully polytheistic view of the Gods for ritual purposes. As such, the beings that form the Three Kindreds are "limited" beings: they are neither omniscient nor omnipresent, so in order to have an effective ritual, we have to get their attention. When we open the Gates, it's something like tugging on the cosmic sleeves of the Kindreds to say, "Hey, here we are, and we're ready to start!" There's some common ritual language that often follows the Gate Opening that sums it up nicely: "We are here to honor the Kindreds." In effect, we're informing the Kindreds that we're going to engage in a conversation with them.

The Gatekeeper is someone who walks between the worlds in mythology. They might often be psychopomps, but that's not the only type of being who can be a Gatekeeper. Often, they are gods of magic, or underworld gods. Sometimes, they are protectors. The Gatekeeper is usually not the same as the deity of the occasion (though he/she can be).

We call on a Gatekeeper because what we're doing in ritual is something best done with the partnership of the gods. By establishing a guest-host relationship with a Gatekeeper, we find protection and guidance through the rite. Sometimes they act as advocate for us, sometimes as transporter of the sacrifice, and sometimes as a generic "opener of ways," providing us with that extra magical *oomph* we need to effect real change in the cosmos.

Theologically speaking, we could open the Gates ourselves (the phrasing "join your magic with ours" is indicative of this), but because our religion is based on that ***ghos-ti-**relationship, why would we want to forgo yet another chance of connecting with the Gods?

For good examples of Gatekeepers, you might think about the Vedic Agni (the quintessential Gatekeeper), the Roman Ianus, or possibly the Norse Heimdallr. For examples of gods filling the "gatekeeper" function like we use it, you might look at the role of the "advocate" gods in Hittite prayers.

Exercise: Opening the Gates of the Heart, Hands, and Mind

This is a simple meditation aimed at helping you open a set of "inner gates" that all of us have, and to learn to do work with the magic that comes from interacting directly with the cosmos. So, read through the exercise, and then try the meditation on your own.

Start by watching your breath for a moment. Feel the air fill and exit your lungs, and seek your center. Once you have your center, it is time to move forward, into the first gate.

Place your hands before you, cupped toward each other, with your right hand over your left. Begin to move them in opposite directions in circular patterns. From your center, connect with the space between your hands. Feel it there, between your hands, as the energy begins to concentrate and expand.

As the energy engulfs your hands, feel the center that your hands now rotate around open. Let it cover your hands with energy, and know that you have the power to work your will in the world, with right action.

Feel both centers: the one at your center, and the one here in your hands. Remember that centers can be separate but the same: your hands and your center are one.

Now, turn your attention to your head. With your hands now full of this power, reach up and touch your forehead and the back of your head. Let the power in your hands expand from front to back, connecting in the center. Here, at this new center, envision a spark that ignites a coal, and it begins to grow.

Let the coal burst into flame, and know as it grows and brightens that this flame is the fire that orders the cosmos, the Fire in the Head. Feel this as a third center, and let this center expand to fill your head, and then open as a gate.

Feel all three centers: your center, your hands, and your head. Remember again that centers can be separate and the same: your hands, your head, and your center are one.

Now, place your hands on your chest, again feeling the power of the gate of the hands. Between your hands, feel a cauldron in your heart. The cauldron is not empty, for it begins to fill with the waters of the earth. Let the cauldron fill until it overflows and runs down your body and back to the earth.

Know that this cauldron is the Cauldron of Creativity, the Bounty of the Waters. Feel the center of that cauldron expand with the waters, letting them flow down your arms and legs. Now, feel those waters as they open as a gate.

Feel again all four centers: your heart, your head, your hands, and your center. All these centers are different, but the same. Now you are centered, powerful, and ready to work in the world. See the fire in the water, feel the warmth of the flame in your hands, feel the waters fill your center: each of these centers brightens and magnifies the others.

Now, begin to close the gates. Place your hands again on your chest, and let the well begin to recede, leaving a coating of water inside you. Touch your head, and let the flame return to a smoldering ash, leaving the warmth of the fire. Rotate your hand in the opposite direction, and feel the center dissipate, leaving your hands energized for the work ahead.

Return to your center, and focus again on your breathing. Return to this realm.

Journal about your experience.

Finding Focus

Learning how to focus your worship is vital when trying to build a personal devotional practice. This focus tends to fall into three distinct categories for every ritual: what we call "Ritual Focus," "Deity Focus," and "Energy Focus," and each focus will provide a different way of looking at the ritual you are doing.

Ritual Focus

The first step in learning what kind of focus to give your rite is learning about the kinds of foci that are available to you. The following chart provides a basic list of types of rites you might find yourself doing. These are after Catherine Bell's work on ritual. There are many other potential categories that rituals might fall into, but this list is neither too exhaustive to be useful, nor so basic that it reduces ritual further than is necessary.

Types of Rituals:

Rites of Passage	**Life cycle or life crisis rites** These rites provide order and definition around the changes in our biological lives
Calendrical and Commemorative Rites	**Periodic, timed, regular rites** Calendrical rites provide order to the passage of time and accompany changes in the seasons, day, or year. Commemorative rites explicitly recall important events
Rites of Exchange and Communication	**Rites of sacrifice, divination, and the union of sacred and profane worlds** These rites focus on the relationship between individuals and sacred beings, and they deal in reciprocity between the two worlds.
Rites of Affliction	**Rites that seek to mitigate the influence of spirits** These rites attempt to rectify a disordered state, including personal misfortune (illness), communal misfortune (famine) or cosmic misfortune (drought), often through purification.
Rites of feasting, fasting, and festival	**Major communal performances that are celebrated publicly and are communally religious in nature** Occasionally, these rites use religious symbolism, but the display may primarily be social in nature, rather than religious

Political Rites	**Rites that promote the power of political institutions** These rites do not uphold the power of political items, but construct that power.

Determining Ritual Focus:

Ritual focus is about the reason for the ritual: what is the purpose, aim, or goal of this ritual? Sometimes, this is simple: if it's October 31st, it's obviously time to honor the Ancestors for the feast of Samhain. Sometimes, though, this is more complicated. You might start by asking yourself these questions, and journaling the answers, and placing the rite into one of the above categories.

- Is this a seasonal rite?
    - What are the common themes in this season?
    - Is there a common working done at this time?
        - Read the lore for this information. You will be surprised what you can learn in just a quick glance through the sources!
- Is this a magical rite?
    - What is the aim you wish to accomplish?
        - We'll cover this again under "energy focus," but think about what you want out of the working.
- Is this a rite of passage?
    - Think about movement: where is the person *coming from*, and where are they *going to*?
        - Rites of passage are often about movement from one place to another, both figuratively and physically. Can the rite of passage be marked by such movement (like the crossing of a bridge, joining another household, or passing through a doorway)?
- Is this a celebration or a ceremony?

- o What is the proper "voice" to speak in? Should you be declarative, reverent, or festive?
  - ▪ "Declarative" rites change the state of the cosmos by saying something "is" or "has become" something else.
  - ▪ "Reverent" rites tend to speak "in awe of" something.
  - ▪ "Festive" rites tend to simply speak joyously about the end result.

Deity Focus

If ritual focus was about the "what," then deity focus is about the "who."

Additionally, calling this "deity focus" is a bit misleading: sometimes, the focus isn't on deities at all, but instead on the Spirits of Nature or the Ancestors, two classes of spirits who are certainly worth honoring with regularity. Again, ask yourself these questions and journal the response. This will help you create invocations and prayers specific to the rite.

Determining Deity Focus:

- What is the focus of your rite?
  - o Are there appropriate spirits for the season, or do deity names appear in the name of the feast?
  - o If this is a rite of passage, is there a spirit (or more than one) who controls the sphere you are leaving or entering?
  - o If this is a celebration, is there a particular spirit appropriate for that celebration?
  - o If you are working a rite of affliction (for instance, seeking health for someone), is there an appropriate spirit to call on?

Energy/Working Focus

If you will be doing any energy-raising or working at all, you must have a reason for it. It is not uncommon in modern Pagan circles to raise energy for the sake of raising energy, but doing this is somewhat irresponsible. Always have a focus if you raise energy.

Determining Energy/Working Focus

- What is the *purpose* of the energy-raising or the working?
- How will you raise the energy?
    o Chanting, toning, and dancing are great options
        - To tone, simply make a sound with your voice. Often, vowel sounds are great for this. As you do so, focus on the energy being raised.
- How will you control it?
    o Closed circle, chant leader, or practice beforehand?
        - Find some sort of focus or "container" for the energy. Often, this can be an object like a jar, crystal, or other item. In large groups, there might be a person who everyone focuses on and they take responsibility for containing the energy.
- How will you release it?
    o Sudden changes in volume (including sudden silence), new sounds, and things being broken or put together are good ways to release the energy.
    o If you gathered the energy in an object, breaking that object is a great way to release the energy, though it is hard to direct.
    o Try to find something that relies on a different sense than the one being used to raise the energy:
        - Toning (auditory) can be released with a visual cue
        - Dancing (tactile) can be released with an audio cue
- How will you ensure that it all goes where it is supposed to?
    o Some people have trouble "letting go" of energy that's been raised. Ease folk along after the working.

Divination and Omen-Taking

We have talked a lot about setting up and preparing for ritual. The next question must be: "How do I know I'm doing it right?" Fortunately, Paganism provides a direct way to ask that question and get a pretty rapid response (in most cases).

Pagan ritual is based not only on the idea that the Kindreds are receptive to our voices, accepting of our gifts, and interested in a relationship with us; but also that they will speak back to us, offer us gifts in return, and continue that relationship with reciprocity. Most importantly, the Kindreds understand us when we communicate with them and have given us ways to understand them when they communicate with us.

Each Pagan ritual calls out to ask the Powers questions about our relationship. These communications take many forms and use many different sorts of symbol sets: ogham, runes, oracle cards, augury, and tarot cards are just a few of the methods that might be used in our rituals.

What is often most important is not necessarily the type of symbol that is used, but an intimate familiarity with the symbols and a knowledge of these symbols that is shared with the Powers. Communication goes two ways: both sides of the conversation must understand not only the symbols used to communicate, but also how those symbols are interpreted by the other side. This means that it is up to us to choose a form appropriate to the Powers and appropriate to ourselves, and to study that form in enough depth that when the symbol is drawn or the bird flies from south to north, we know and understand the message as it is intended to be understood.

Most often, when we ask questions, we are asking three basic types of questions of the Kindreds:

- Acceptance: "Has our sacrifice been accepted?" "Has this been pleasing unto the Gods?"
- Clarification: "What more can we do?" "What do you bring for us?"
- Blessings: "What further blessings do the Kindreds offer?" "What is offered to us in turn?"

Book 1 – Ritual Foundations

There are several methods of taking an omen in ritual, and the questions vary from Grove to Grove and even Pagan to Pagan. Most will ask three questions. Three Cranes Grove, ADF, uses this set:

1. Have our offerings been accepted?
2. What blessings do the Powers offer in return?
3. What further needs do the Powers have of us?

We have asked these questions because they seem to get us the most detailed answers we can possibly seek. We hear from the Powers not only whether the ritual went well, but what blessings we might receive in the cup and any further instruction they may have to give. It is because of the breadth of response that is possible that our Grove has stuck with this format.

Other Groves ask a different series of questions, which changes the focus of the ritual a bit:

1. What blessings do the Ancestors offer us?
2. What blessings do the Nature Spirits offer us?
3. What blessings do the Shining Ones offer us?

The above three questions start with the assumption that the Powers have accepted the sacrifices given, and will be offering blessings in return for the gifts.

Hemlock Vales Protogrove, ADF, settled on a hybrid, in which four questions are asked of the Kindreds:

1. Have our offerings been accepted?
2. What blessings do the Ancestors offer us?
3. What blessings do the Nature Spirits offer us?
4. What blessings do the Shining Ones offer us?

This, of course, solves the issues with the alternate three questions listed above, and also dispenses with the "three question" format that is so popular (sometimes, it's nice that things don't always come in three's).

For our Grove's Druid Moon rituals, we ask a different set of three questions, ones designed to learn different things about our Grove:

1. What is our Path?
2. On what should the Grove focus until the next Druid Moon?
3. On what should each individual focus until the next Druid Moon?

The idea with these questions was to look at how we have done in the past, consider where we are going as a Grove in the future, and think about how we, as individuals, can do work in our own lives for the next month.

Remember, too, that negative responses should always be considered a very real possibility. Resist the urge to turn a negative omen into a positive one, and always go with your first instinct. For a very frightening omen, you might think about flipping coins. Nothing says "honesty" like increasing the odds for a negative omen!

This communication aspect of Druidic ritual is very much dependent on the tenet of "hard polytheism," which says that we deal with the Powers as individuals, not as collectives or as parts of ourselves. The individual Powers have the ability to communicate with us and express their opinions and enhance their relationships with us through a set of symbols we share. Also, this is another "ritual assumption" that is integral to how our rituals work. However you see divination (as communication with your own subconscious mind, as a way to tap into the akashic records, or any other of a number of theories), in our rituals divination is between ourselves and the Powers is very much a real communication with real beings, where we ask a question and we receive an answer.

Ritual Clothing, Jewelry, and Props

"Props" is a deliberate word choice for the heading of this section: we may refer to most everything from our robes to our wand as "tools," but in the end they are theatrical props. That is not to discount the importance of robes, flags, cups, wands, and other ritual tools on the focus and flow of the spiritual energies. The Pope in his robes, the president in the oval office, a flag draped over a coffin, or a witch standing and pointing her wand at the sky all are sign posts for the unconscious mind and help elicit and direct spiritual and emotion responses from the participates.

A key thing to remember is that modern Paganism is what we like to call a "fire religion." By this we mean that fire is central to our rituals and is pretty much ever-present. In light of that, plan your wardrobe accordingly! Remember, ritual robes should not be flammable, have droopy sleeves that might brush a candle, or have dangling stoles that might end up in a ritual fire!

It is important to understand why you have certain tools and know how to use them. We won't spend much time on this subject but understand that ritual tools are just those tools to aid you in your spiritual and magical work and should be treated as sacred objects. Many of us have been in the middle of ritual at home or on the run and grabbed any two bowl and stick to perform ritual, but we should never disregard the importance of having special sacred objects that have been consecrated for just spiritual work.

One thing that you should certainly remember about tools is that it is easy to have too many or too few—and *very* hard to balance what you truly need!

When you are setting up, only put ritual tools out that you **a)** will need, and **b)** have a place for. If you need it and don't have a place for it, make a place for it; if, however, you didn't think about making a place for an item, consider strongly whether you actually *need* it.

Understand that matching props and matching clothing conveys authority and togetherness: if you are working with someone, it will help both of you (and later, as we get into public practice, everyone else!) get into a stronger ritual mind-set, and it will help you "suspend disbelief" about what you are doing, too.

When you pack your ritual tools, make sure that the ones you need in ritual are accessible: have your offerings handy and any other tools available quickly. Nothing is worse than having to fumble for something in the middle of a prayer.

A word or two on jewelry: wear it only if you need it. There is a lot of "Pagan bling" out there, and most of it isn't required for ritual. Be honest with yourself about what you are wearing and why you put it on.

Also, think about others when selecting ritual clothing and jewelry: when you start working with others, you might find that not everyone shares your views on certain ritual symbols, or on fur/leather in ritual. It is wise to respect others you wish to work with on a permanent basis. A common item among Norse folks and some Vedics is the swastika. No matter what the original intent of the symbol was, or how long it was associated with positive energy, some people have a violent reaction to it. Accepting that some symbols have been sullied beyond reclamation in public can be hard, but it is also necessary if you wish to work with others in peace.

Exercise: Praying to Your Tools

An excellent exercise is to pray to your ritual tools. It may sound strange, but by recognizing that the tool we use in ritual has an animate spirit, we recognize that it has *power* as well: a tool that you are not willing to pray to is not a tool that will serve you well.

To do this exercise, you may wish to find a partner, but you can do it alone as well. We have included instructions for both:

Praying to Your Own Tools

Begin with the tool you wish to pray to: a wand, a cup, a tarot deck... all are suitable. Look at it for a moment and think about the tool. Ask yourself: Does it have a name? What has it done before? Is it new or old, and what are your hopes for it or how has it been good to you? What does it mean to you?

Once you have thought about three key points, pray to the tool with a prayer of praise. Tell it how great it is.

Now, look at the tool again and journal for a bit about how you feel about it, now that you have prayed to it.

Praying to Someone Else's Tools

Each of you should tell about the tool you have chosen. Tell a story about how you used it in a ritual, or where you found it. Explain its significance, and tell the other person its name (if it has one).

Now, trade tools, and pray a prayer of praise to each other's tools in turn.

Write about how you feel now that someone else has recognized the animate spirit in your ritual tool.

Blessing Your Tools

A step beyond the exercise of praying to your tools is to formally bless the tool. Much like the purification process, you will want to use fire and water to purify the item, and you will want to pray over the tool, as well.

One tool in heavy use in our Grove is the Crane Bag. This is a bag that a Druid keeps their ritual tools in: it can be large or small, simple or elegant. We have included an example working for consecrating a Crane Bag here; it is a bit more complicated than a simple purification and prayer, but it may provide ideas of what more you may wish to do in such a rite.

Consecrating your ritual tools is a way of cleansing and charging them for the work they will aid you in. **"Consecrate"** simply means setting aside, claiming or hallowing an item as sacred. Below is an example of how an Order of the Crane member might consecrate their Crane Bag.

Example: Consecrating the Crane Bag

If you carry a crane bag, you may wish to consecrate it. To that end, we provide here a working that will fit into a daily devotion, just after you have affirmed the return flow and you are filled with the power of the Spirits (it will go in the "working" section of the rite, for reference). You will need three candles and a small portion of the Waters of Life that you blessed in the ritual, so remember to hold some back (you may wish to keep an extra cup or bowl on your altar to contain these waters).

The Crane Bag Working

When you have come to that portion of the rite where you are prepared to consecrate your crane bag, place the bag (or bags, if you are consecrating more than one) upon your altar in the center of three unlit candles.

When you are prepared to begin, speak these words as you light the candles:

This crane bag is an outward symbol of my work. I bring it here, into the presence of the Kindreds, to consecrate it and bless it for the work to come.

(light the first candle)

With this candle lit, I bring the light of my hearth and all who share it in hospitality!

(light the second candle)

With this candle lit, I bring the light of my integrity, that I may work in wholeness with the artful cosmos!

(light the third candle)

With this candle lit, I bring the light of vision and banish darkness, that I may know the way with the guidance of the Crane!

Now, draw forth the Waters of Life you had set aside, and speak these words:

I call out to the Kindreds to let the blessings from my devotion fall upon this crane bag, that it be ever ready to help me as I walk the path of the Crane.

(sprinkle water upon the bag)

Now with this blessing of fire and water joining here, I pray that the Kindreds hear my prayer and make this bag blessed in their sight:

> Manannan made it,
> Oisin received it from his hand.
> Lugh carried it,
> The sons of Caermade stole it.
> Manannan retrieved it,
> And Conaire received it.
> Though treachery was its start,
> It guarded its magic treasures well.
> Full at high tide, empty at low,
> This bag is the cunning-folk's hoard.
> Let it transform me though wearing
> The Crane who guides me through worlds.

Now, put the crane bag on, and wear it with pride. Thank those who have helped you (we recommend thanking Mannanan for the crane bag, and the Crane for his blessings) and close the gates.

Keys to Props and Locations

It's always difficult to figure out exactly what you need and exactly what sorts of things to look for in a location. These tips should help you plan your rituals, whether you're just starting or you've been doing this for some time.

- **Start with a checklist** – This is the simplest, but most often overlooked idea to make your ritual preparation go smoothly and consistently. Include common items that you need to buy or replace every time.
- **Keep your hallows (sacred things) in one place** – It is often good to create a laminated list of your hallows items to keep with the hallows. Our Grove keeps our hallows in a large rubber tub so that we know where everything is (and because we take them from place to place). In your home, you might choose instead to put them in a nice cabinet.
- **Consider different checklists for different rites** – Not all rites are created equal, and sometimes you need different things: at Imbolc, you need candles, and at

Samhain you might need an ancestor box. This is especially helpful as you build traditions around the High Days.
- **Not every rite may be in the same place** – Perhaps you want to be out in the woods, or you want to rent a nice cabin from a local park. When scouting locations look for:
    - Ability to have fire or other necessary ritual items (review location of smoke alarms and windows, too!)
    - Ambient noise that might disrupt a rite, including freeways, airplanes, trains, etc.
- **Ensure that you have planned enough time for the rite** – Remember that ritual is not just "reading from the page:" you will have actions and movements that will add to the time you need
- **After every ritual, clean your ritual gear!**

Summary of Ritual Props

Think about what you are wearing, and

Props and costumes are great for setting the mood, creating ritual drama, and directing energy but common sense should always override. No one wants to be remembered as the really cool Roman who showed up in a toga in December and lost his toes to frostbite and nothing disrupts a ritual as someone's nice flowing robe going up in flames as they give an offering to the fire. Everyone should dress weather appropriate and be mindful of flammable materials and props.

Exercises for Building Personal Ritual Work

Always start with a checklist so you know what to bring!

A Sample Ritual Checklist

High Day:_____   Comment:

Script/Notes	
Hallows	
Chant Sheets	
Water for Well/Blessing	
Firewood	
First Aid Kit	
Fire Extinguisher	
Table(s) for Altar, etc.	
Table Clothes	
Altar Décor	
Offerings	
-Kindred Offerings	
-Earth Mother Offerings	
-Key Offerings	
-Special Offerings	
Banner	
Handouts (ADF, GROVE, etc.)	
Raffle Tickets/Prizes	
Lighter/Matches	
Flashlight	
Bottle Opener	
Scissors	
Bilé (tree representation)	
Other Props:	

Speaking in Ritual

Whether we are in public or in private, it is right to come before the gods with our voices proud and strong. In the ancient world, silent prayer was often outlawed because religion was a civic responsibility: you came to the temple and did your work out loud, because anyone who comes before the gods must do so with a pure heart: someone unwilling to give voice to their prayers was at least as likely to be doing evil magic or praying to take away the good from their neighbors as they were to pray for the health of society.

To that end, we encourage you to always pray out loud at your altar, and to speak as if you are not alone; after all, as we have mentioned before, you are not: the Kindreds hear your words when spoken.

Because of this, we need to focus for a bit on how we present ourselves in ritual, including how we speak. Much of this will be particularly useful in public ritual, but for now we will focus on the things that make the most sense in personal ritual (always pointing out where they are helpful in public ritual as well, if it isn't obvious).

Preparation

Relaxation

Relaxation is where we must start. A relaxed ritualist is open and able to speak and move with confidence. A tense ritualist is always constrained. Focus wanders, distractions abound, and, frankly, it shows. Warm-up techniques for both the body and voice will go a long way towards relaxation, such as shaking the arms and legs, bouncing on the balls of the feet, stretching the muscles, even running in place. Vocal exercises will limber up the voice and make it more free and effective. Mental relaxation can be achieved through meditation, slow, deep breathing, and concentration on items in your vicinity. Relaxation is not zoning out, going into a stupor or just being a bag of bones, rather it is a calm, receptive openness to everything around you.

Before rituals led by a group of celebrants, it is also a good idea to attune to the Powers and to each other, through the use of the 2 Powers meditation or other techniques. This preparation, on top of the ones mentioned earlier in this section, will aid in your relaxation.

Posture

Posture is very important for the ritualist. Not only will good posture make you look good, giving you more presence and authority, but it will also help make your voice stronger and more resonant. Take off your clothes and have a good long look in the mirror. Stand with your sides to the mirror and see how straight you are standing. Usually, most of us slouch to some extent or another.

Exercise: Improving Your Posture

A really good way to improve your posture is to imagine that a string is attached to the top of your head. Then imagine, and clearly see in your mind's eye, that some God or Goddess is gently pulling up on that string. Keep your shoulders relaxed, and feel yourself straighten up, led by that string attached to your head. Then try walking around keeping the same feeling. Practice this regularly for a while and see the difference in how you feel.

This posture exercise can also be a good psychic cue for you at the beginning of a rite, helping you put yourself into sacred space and time. Or you can just allow yourself have good posture all the time!

Trust

You have to trust both yourself and your fellow ritualists. Without this trust, you will be constantly on your guard and your focus will suffer. Trust is not a passive thing – it must be actively sought out. Reach out to your fellow ritualists and determine ways to work together. Should one of them prove not to be completely trustworthy, create strategies to cope with any situations you can foresee. To be able to trust yourself, you must prepare yourself, mentally and physically, for the tasks ahead. And this will require discipline. See the section on Stage Fright below for some trust exercises you can do.

Discipline

Without discipline there can be no trust between collaborators, and group ritual is a collaborative art. Be on time for any rehearsals and for the ritual itself – coming forth to lead others to honor the Kindreds is not a casual activity. It is one of the greatest importance.

Self-discipline is also required for success. Learn those invocations, warm up your body and voice, do what it takes to be totally prepared. Take the time to do what is required.

Freedom

The ritualist also must learn to be free – free from inhibitions that could stifle the work. And the ritualist must learn to enjoy this freedom – ritual is serious stuff, but it need not be solemn (Cohen, 5-24). Even within the most scripted rite the Spirits may touch you, prompting you to veer off course for a moment, giving the rite an added spark or joyous touch. Enjoy those moments of divine contact, but remember that freedom must be tempered with responsibility, so get back on track when the moment has passed.

Enthusiasm

When we make our invocations, deep inside we know that the Spirits will answer us. When we have made relationships with Them, They actually do care about us, and actively wish us well. So approach the work with a positive expectation that you *will* be successful in what you do. Speak directly *to* Them. *Know* that They will come. Doing this will also help the ritualist avoid self-consciousness (Cohen, 57). After all, you're not really speaking to the empty air, or just to the folks attending the ritual (though you are speaking to them as well). You are speaking to the Kindreds themselves.

The Voice

Vocal Production

Very simply, after we inhale, filling our lungs with air by use of the diaphragmatic and intercostal (rib) muscles, the excitor muscles (those muscles that control the supply of air we exhale so that sound can happen) get it all started. The controlled flow of air passes through a vibrator (the vocal cords), which produces sound as the air passes across it. These sounds are amplified and broadened by the resonators (cavities in the chest, throat, mouth and nose). These resonators affect how the voice sounds, giving it a tone unique to each individual (Elizabeth, 9).

OK, enough of that technical stuff. Let's get down to brass tacks here.

The Breath

The voice is probably the most important tool a ritualist can have for presentational work. And the breath is the basis of the voice. The ritualist's goal is simply to breathe naturally while under the pressure of leading ritual, and to supply enough power to support the voice in difficult circumstances, such as working outdoors (Cohen, 113).

Have you ever watched a baby cry? They have yet to learn the bad habits of our culture, and so breathe naturally and fully, bringing forth enough sound to shake the windows, and with apparently little effort. Notice how they breathe – deeply and fully from the base of their abdomens. They don't visibly fill their chests – most action appears to take place in the area of the stomach. This is because when people inhale, the air is sucked into the lungs by the motion of the diaphragm, which pulls down on the lungs (as well as the action of the intercostals which expand the chest). This motion of the diaphragm causes the stomach to distend, or appear to push out. The person is not pushing his/her stomach out, rather it is simply getting out of the way of the diaphragm. In like manner, when the person exhales, the diaphragm pushes upwards on the lungs and the intercostals contract, making the chest cavity smaller. This may appear as if the stomach were being pulled in.

When we yawn, we not only relax the throat but we automatically breathe from the base of the abdomen. This also occurs when we are sleeping. The trick for the ritualist is to re-learn how to do this when awake and working in ritual.

Exercise: Breathing from the Abdomen

Lie down on your back on the floor, knees raised and feet flat on the floor. Place one hand on your stomach and one hand on your chest. Breathe normally, paying close attention to your body and your hands. Is your chest moving? Is your stomach moving?

Place your awareness under the hand on your stomach. Breathe deeply again and "see" the air filling the cavity under that hand, passing through the chest without stopping. Did the hand on your belly rise? Did the hand on your chest remain mostly still?

Practice this a few times until you can get your breath to fill deeply within you. If you're having problems getting this to happen, try consciously pushing out your stomach while inhaling, keeping your chest still. (Remember, the inflow of the air is not caused by pushing out the stomach, but by the action of the diaphragm). Try this a few times until you sense the movement of the diaphragm filling the lungs. It can be a subtle difference.

Exercise: The Yawn

Place the tip of your tongue against the inside of your lower front teeth. Open your mouth and expand your throat, and then inhale. This should lead you to yawn organically. Let the yawn flow naturally through you. This relaxes the throat and helps make vocal production easier.

Breath Support

Strengthening the muscles that control and support the breath is essential for the production of strong and directed sound. Just doing vocalizations can achieve this, but there are exercises that can help achieve and maintain this support.

First of all, we all need to have a strong core to our bodies. Only by strengthening our core can we have strong and effective vocal production. Our core is the basis of all we do – be it walk, dance, speak, sing, even have sex. And the best and easiest way to strengthen the core of the body is to do crunches. In the old days, folks were advised to do sit-ups, but we know now that the old-fashioned sit-up can actually cause lower back problems, so don't bother with those.

Exercise: Basic Crunches

As with the 'Breathing From the Abdomen' exercise above, lie on your back on the floor with your knees up and feet flat on the floor. Place your hands behind your neck and interlace your fingers.

As you exhale, tighten your stomach muscles and slowly lift your shoulders off of the floor. Only raise them a few inches or so off the floor – don't go too far. When you reach that raised position, hold for a moment and then slowly lower yourself again. Repeat. Be careful that you don't pull on your neck with your hands – they are only there to support the weight of your head.

At first you may only be able to do a few of these, and that's fine. Keep working at them on successive days until you can do 25 or so in a row. That's probably enough for one session. Do a session of crunches regularly – daily is best (of course) but two or three times a week is probably adequate.

Now that you've begun strengthening your core, it's time to start working those diaphragm muscles. Here is a very effective exercise that works for most people.

Exercise 5: Explosive Breathing

Stand upright and relax your body, particularly your shoulders. Perform and Yawn exercise to relax your throat. Breathe deeply into your abdomen while staying relaxed. When ready, quickly contract your diaphragm and stomach muscles, forcing the air out of your lungs quickly and explosively. ***HAH*** **DO NOT USE YOUR VOICE OR TIGHTEN YOUR THROAT.** This is just an explosive, voiceless out-flowing of air in a relaxed throat.

Repeat this, making the exhalations closer and closer together, allowing yourself a short inhalation between each exhalation if necessary.

Be careful not to hyperventilate! Concentrate on the rapid contraction of the diaphragm and stomach muscles. ***HAH. HAH. HAH. HAH. HAH.*** Rest for a moment, and try it again.

How can you know if you have a strong and well-controlled breathing apparatus? One easy way is to do the following exercise.

Exercise: Continuous Tones while Jumping

Make a single, continuous sound, like singing a single note, and start jumping up and down. Does the sound wobble or does it sound the same as when you were standing still? When you have a strong core and vocal apparatus, the tone should be as steady while jumping, as it is when you are standing still.

Pitch Range

Pitch is the actual note that we use when speaking. Normally, most people speak within a range of a few notes, but when excited, the range of notes used in speech can increase. Listen to someone shout from a distance and you'll hear a difference (Cohen, 118).

Higher notes tend to resonate in the head, and lower notes in the chest and throat, but everyone is different. One thing that the aspiring ritualist needs to remember, however, is that it can be harmful to try and speak outside of your normal pitch range. Sometimes, for instance, a man may believe that in order to sound more 'manly', he needs to speak using lower notes. This is called *under pitching*, and can damage the voice. The way to have a deeper, richer voice is to *resonate* more in the chest, not lower the pitch.

Exercise 7: Exploring Your Pitch Range

Breathe from the abdomen and pick a note in your normal range. Then speak each of the following lines on that note (and this time, do use your voice):

a.   hah hah hah hah hah hah hah

b.   bah bah bah bah bah bah bah

c.   pah pah pah pah pah pah pah

Now pick a lower note in your range, and repeat the above lines.
Pick a higher note in your range and repeat. You can do this with all the notes you can muster to see what your speaking range is like.
REMEMBER – you are speaking, not singing.

Now do the following, sliding down the scale from top to bottom. Repeat, rising up the scale from bottom to top:

d.   ahhhhhhhhhhhhhhhhhhhhhhhhhhhhh
(Cohen, 115)

Resonance

When we make sounds with our vocal cords, certain tissues and cavities in our bodies make sympathetic vibrations, increasing the amount and affecting the quality of the sound we produce. Imagine striking a tuning fork and placing it on a wooden box – the sound you hear will be amplified tremendously (Cohen, 115). This is called *resonance*. And this is something we can do with our own bodies. Different vowel and consonantal sounds will resonate in different areas – and we can also focus our sound in different resonating cavities. The main areas of resonance are the face and nose, the throat and the chest.

Americans and Canadians tend to 'speak' in their throats, while Europeans tend to 'speak' in their faces (also called the *mask*). Resonating in the mask will act to carry your voice much further than resonating in your throat. Resonating in the chest will give your voice a deeper and richer quality.

But how do we get our voices to resonate in these places? Well, we all probably know one facial resonance spot – the nasal cavities. Most of us can, at will, put our voices in our noses and make that 'nasal' sound that sounds pretty funny. But this sound, when added to the resonances possible in the rest of the mask, can add a lot to the beauty and strength of the voice.

Exercise 8: Resonating in the Nose and Mask

a. Stand comfortably but with good posture, and relax. Make a sustained *ng* sound (like the *ng* in the word *sing*). Feel the vibrations in the top and back of your nose.

b. Now make a sustained sound of the letter *m*. *Mmmmmmmmmm*. Feel how the vibrations have moved down to your lips. Play with the sound, going back and forth between the *ng* and *m* sounds.

c. Now start with the m sound again. Open your mouth and turn the *m* sound into *mahhhhhhhhh*. Go back to the single *m* sound with your mouth closed again. Repeat a few times.

In doing part c. of the above exercise, you may find your voice retreating back into your throat once you release the *m* sound and go into the *ah* sound. Keep practicing this until you can keep the entire sound in your mask, with it vibrating all through your face. Be aware, though, that the quality of the sound will be different when there is a vowel involved.

d. Repeat part c. of this exercise using different vowels, and feel where the vibrations take place.

While chest resonance is particularly important for men, it is useful for women as well, at least in the speaking (as opposed to the singing) voice. It adds depth and strength to any voice. The sound may be subtler in women than it is in men, however.

Exercise 9: Resonating in the Chest

Have you ever blown over the top of a bottle and made it sing a note? That's the same principle that chest resonance uses. In this exercise we will be attempting to recreate a similar sound using our own chest cavity instead of a bottle.

Sit in a comfortable chair, drop your shoulders and relax. Do the yawn exercise a couple of times to open and relax the throat.

Open your mouth and throat, inhale, and with a breathy voice say,

"*Oh hum, I'm so tired! Ooooooooooooooooo*"

while slowly dropping your head and bending over in your seat, shaking your head side to side. (Note: the *Oooooo* sound should rhyme with the word, *boot*.)

Practice this often. When I learned this technique, it took me two weeks of steady practice to finally hear a difference in my voice, so don't despair!

Speech

Diction and Enunciation (Articulation)

In the old days, before Method Acting became popular in films (think Marlon Brando), diction was seen as critical for good performances. Indeed, on the stage this is still the case, but it isn't so important in everyday life, and many people have speech that is quite sloppy. Mumbling and imprecise diction are the norm, but while this may be fine for day-to-day conversation, it's deadly on the stage or in ritual. There, words have to be heard across distance, and distance distorts sound a little bit. This distortion seems to increase with distance, and when it's not possible to see the lips of the person speaking, it can be even worse. Add in differences of accent or dialect and the entire edifice falls down around our ears.

We may call this lack of clarity on the part of a speaker as 'mush-mouth'.

As a ritualist, it is your job to be heard and understood. Good diction, mixed in with vocal projection, will succeed every time. So it pays to give your actual speech mechanics a bit of your time and attention.

Are you aware that in American English, internal *t*'s often get pronounced as *d*'s? *Butter* becomes *budder*, *wetter* becomes *wedder*. In British English, some dialects have intrusive *r*'s. When a word ends with a vowel and the next word begins with a vowel, the letter *r* may get stuck in the middle - "*Asia and Africa*" becomes "*Asia/r/ and Africa*". These dialectical differences can be charming, but it's best to be aware of your own personal habits.

Exercise 10: Demosthenes Revisited

The great Athenian orator Demosthenes was said to have had a stutter as a child, which he overcame by practicing his speeches with a mouth full of pebbles. Here is a variation on that theme:

Put a pencil between your upper and lower teeth, with the ends sticking out on either side of your face. While holding the pencil securely, read a piece of text (like, say, a paragraph from this essay), taking care to enunciate each word clearly. This is excellent practice for the lips and tongue.

Exercise 11: Tongue Twisters

Tongue twisters are a great way to practice your diction and avoid the terrors of mush-mouth. Start slowly with the examples below and then speed up with practice (Elizabeth, 225):

a. Peter picked a pint of pickled peppers. *(repeat)*

b. Rubber baby buggy bumpers. *(repeat)*

c. Six sleek swans swam swiftly southwards. *(repeat)*

d. Lovely lemon liniment. *(repeat)*

e. The great Greek grape growers grow great Greek grapes.

f. Toy boat, toy boat, toy boat. *(repeat)*

Using the Voice

Liberating the Voice

Many of us have been conditioned by society to be polite in social situations, sometimes even timid or deferential. Now, even the most outgoing person will occasionally experience a moment of qualm when, say, the entire room turns and looks at him/her, but in ritual *everyone* will be looking at you, so you will need to train yourself to let yourself go. As a celebrant your voice needs to explode, to excite, to be warm and bright. It is essential that the ritualist break down these repressive hang-ups so that s/he may, at will, do what is needed.

Exercise 12: Rude Words

The purpose of this exercise is to get over saying rude words without giggling or releasing your discomfort in any other way. This may help you find the courage you might need to liberate your voice. Of course, if these words are part of your normal vocabulary this may not work. Allow your voice to say, at full volume and with clear speech, the sort of words you don't normally get to say in public (Cohen, 130). Speak the following with feeling:

a. Shit, shit, shit, shit, shit!
b. Penis, penis, penis, penis!
c. Fuck, fuck, fuck, fuck, fuck!

d. Asshole, asshole, asshole, asshole, asshole! (for our British friends, you might try saying *arsehole* instead)
e. Testicle, testicle, testicle, testicle, testicle!
f. Masturbate, masturbate, masturbate, masturbate, masturbate!

Vocal Warm-ups

It's always best to warm up the voice before any ritual. This will help prevent hoarseness and make your voice sound the best it can.

Exercise 13: **Basic Vocal Warm-ups**

These were taught to me when I played the role of Harold Hill in *The Music Man*. These warm-ups, stolen from singers, enabled me to get through a long and arduous vocal part.

a. First, yawn (see Exercise 3 above)
b. Keeping your throat open, as in a yawn, gently say **ah** with a breathy voice without holding a note. Make the sound for your entire exhalation.
c. Using a keyboard, if possible, pick a note that you are comfortable with, in the middle of your range.
d. Gently sing **ah**, moving up five pitches and back down again (for instance, if you started on middle C, gently sing **ah** on C, then D, then E, then F, then G, and reverse the process coming back down again).
e. Repeat, but start on the next note up the scale (that would be D in my example above). Repeat, going up a note for your start until you reach the top of your range – **do not strain** to hit high notes – stop when you are no longer singing freely and comfortably.
f. Now go back to your first starting note (middle C in my example above) and repeat. Repeat again, but go down a note for your starting note

and repeat until you reach the bottom of your range. Again, do not strain the voice.

g. Now repeat the entire process again, but this time use the sound ***mah*** (this brings the sound forward into your mask). You may then play with these sounds, using ***moh***, ***meh***, ***mee***, ***moo***, etc. (Note: the *ee* sound is more difficult to produce on higher notes because of the way it can tighten the back of the mouth – don't strain!)

TIP – Keeping the Voice Lubricated

When in ritual (and when warming up), your voice may start to feel dry. Before ritual begins, be sure that you are well hydrated. During ritual, ***sip*** only tepid (lukewarm or body temperature) water. This will help to keep your voice lubricated.

NOTE - Avoid warm and cold water, teas, honey, throat lozenges, etc. as these will fool you into thinking that your throat is feeling better when in actuality they are only deadening pain, which can lead to strain or overuse of the voice. Also, avoid any milk products for a few hours before ritual as they cause phlegm in the throat and sinuses.

Projection

Projection is the art of making your voice reach to all corners of your ritual space in as effortless a manner as possible. While this can also mean, "raise the volume", it must be stressed that you should accomplish this through resonance and not by 'pushing' the voice.

Bring all your practice of breath support, pitch and resonance together as one, and this will enable you to properly project your voice. Indoors, this is relatively easy, once you master the basics, but outdoors can be tricky even for the most experienced of us (see below).

How loud is loud enough? This is a common question, and one that you will probably have to learn through experience. However, while indoors, you can judge your volume by how it sounds to you, and this can help you learn to feel your volume kinesthetically, through your body, so that you don't overdo it when outdoors.

Exercise 14: Bouncing Your Voice Off the Walls

a. In the shower –

Stand in the shower and yawn (don't inhale the water!). Breathe from your abdomen and place your voice in your mask by doing the *M* and *Mah* sounds exercise in 8.c. above. Then say,

"Once more into the breech, dear friends, once more!
Or close the wall up with English dead!"

This line can sound quite loud in this tiny space. Hear the resonance in your voice. Try it again at a different volume, first quieter, and the next time try is louder. Judge how much effort it took to make the sound 'just right'.

b. In a small room –

This time, prepare as usual, standing in the middle of a small room, and speak the line as before. Find the volume that sounds a bit louder than normal conversation. This is probably the ideal amount of projection for this space.

c. In a large room –

Do the same as before, but in a much larger room, or on a stage in a theatre. Can you hear your voice come back to you from the back wall? Can you judge just how much volume is required to be heard well in this space? Get a friend to go to the other end of the room and listen to you speak. Can s/he hear you loudly and clearly? Again, take care not to strain your voice.

Movement in Ritual

Intentional Movement

Most often, we want people to know what we're doing when we move: we want to be clear that we are consecrating the Waters, or that we are opening the Gates. Sometimes our movements are meant to show others how to move, as well: the manner in which we approach the icon is meant to show others how to approach, or the direction we face when appeasing the Outdwellers is an example to others. If we are able to let people know what we are doing and why we are doing it through movement alone (without wasted or meaningless movement), this is "intentional movement."

The Importance of Intentional Movement

Public ritual is full of movement, from start to finish: the priest moves her hands over the Waters of Life to consecrate them, the congregation moves into the sacred space from outside the grove, and the individual walks to the fire to make sacrifice as well as to sing praise. All of these movements have an obvious purpose to both the person doing them and the congregation who watches them.

Walking in circles or making complicated movements with your body placement constantly changes the direction your voice is projecting. Spiraling to the center may have a lovely effect on your own trance work, but it leaves nearly everyone else in the circle distracted by the change in your voice, both in terms of volume and due to a slight Doppler effect. Fiddling with your fingers or shifting your weight from foot to foot will often remove the focus of your audience from your invocation and direct it to the "odd thing" you are doing.

Taking the time to not only work through your speaking parts, but also to consider the hand motions and body language is vital. Practice making sacrifices to a real fire, and listen to how the piece of silver you bought sounds when it strikes the bottom of your well. If you count on it to go correctly when you do it the first time, you're more than likely making a mistake. By practicing the movements, they will become more fluid, and will appear to come more naturally during ritual.

Nothing appears more reverent in a ritual than someone acting carefully and deliberately.

Exercise: Choreographing a Prayer

Now that we know that words and motion go together, it is time to consider what we might do with a single prayer: how might our actions amplify our words, and how might our words amplify our actions?

For this exercise, we have chosen a simple prayer by Ceisiwr Serith (I'll take a moment to plug his books, *A Book of Pagan Prayer* and *A Pagan Ritual Prayer Book*, both must-owns for the modern Pagan, regardless of tradition). This is a commonly-spoken prayer at Three Cranes Grove, ADF:

> The Waters support and surround us,
> The Land extends about us,
> The Sky stretches out above us;
> At our center, burns a living flame.
> May all the Kindreds bless us.
> May our worship be true,
> May our actions be just,
> May our love be pure.
> Blessings, Honor, and Worship to the Holy Ones

Say the prayer a few times, then start to visualize how you think the words should be accompanied by gestures or movements. Once you have it figured out in your mind, say it with the actions and see how they feel.

Eventually, you will find a set of actions that have meaning to you.

Developing Group Rituals

Praying in public can be a bit daunting, especially if you have only ever prayed privately to the Kindreds before. Here are a few key things to remember about group work that can help you transition from working inwardly to working with others.

Prayer in Public Spaces

Making the transition from private, personal ritual to public ritual can be complicated, but there are a few short principles that can help smooth that transition.

1) **Public prayer is external, communal and celebratory.** This is not silent, personal prayer, but rather external, loud prayer. When you speak the words of public prayer, you will not be speaking on your behalf, but on the behalf of the community. To that end, you must remember to speak at a volume where everyone can hear and understand you. Additionally, remember that you are speaking praise for all in attendance, and that praise should be celebratory, not apologetic or fearful.

2) **Speaking in liturgy is a leadership role.** By agreeing to speak on behalf of others, you are accepting a leadership role. Part of that responsibility is to understand the Folk, and to channel that understanding into what is said. Often, it is easy to feel that we are speaking about our **personal** understanding of a being. Instead, we should offer a broader understanding whenever possible.

3) **Public prayer is a time to reveal the beings.** Who is this being we are honoring, and what does he or she (or what do they) look like? Draw on pieces of myth and weave them into your words, describe what a god looks like, or where a goddess lives; but describe these things not as "features," but as reflections of what they *do*. Describe how they are related to us, and why these particular beings are appropriate to the rite done today. People love to hear the stories of their deities again and again because the stories are *their* stories, so treat public prayer more as a way to reveal this being to the folk again for the very first time.

4) **Public prayer is not a time to teach or lecture.** It can be easy to try to provide a deep lesson about the being or beings called, but remember that this is praise, not a time to remind people of fault or shortcomings. It can be tempting to single out an aspect that relates to someone in your Grove, such as how Mitra is a god of oaths and should not be crossed if someone has broken an oath, or how the Dagda got drunk and paid the price if someone fell off the wagon. The rule of thumb here is that if you think of someone that this can be directed at, don't use it in ritual.

5) **Know how to stand and how to move.** Know where and in what position you will stand, and how you will move to that place and any other places you may need to move to. Know where your offering is, when you will pick it up, and what to do with it when the sacrifice is made. If you will be reading, practice reading and the motions of offering at the same time.

Remember, when we pray in public, we pray with our whole being, and our physical presence is just as important, because it shows others our spiritual presence.

Projection Outdoors

Many Pagan rites are conducted outdoors, and this can be very hard on the voice because it is so very difficult to judge your projection and volume when outside. There are no walls to bounce your voice off of, and it just keeps going past the congregation and out into the world.

For this reason *it is critical* that you practice your voice indoors and learn kinesthetically what different volumes feel like. Then, while outside, the voice can be set at the volume needed for a large room, *and no more*, to prevent hoarseness and vocal fatigue. In time, you will learn to trust your body and voice to do what you need them to do.

Building Group Cohesion

Familiarity in Ritual

- **Knowledge:** Spend time studying and practicing with others. A key factor in building cohesion is "agreeing on the cosmological situation." If everyone agrees that there are three Kindreds; three Realms; that the fire, well and tree can be Gates to the cosmos; and that the deities can hear us and respond through an omen, then you will find the group is already very cohesive.

- **Affection:** Having a positive working relationship and mutual respect goes a long way: it reduces the fear of "screwing up;" builds trust; and lessens the impact of mistakes, should they occur.

- **Group Identity:** Building a group identity happens over time: it starts with agreeing to be a part of a group. Give it a name (preferably one that can be more than a name) and have regular meetings. View this group as a team, not a group of friends who get together. It may sound a bit silly, but wearing the same color of clothing, similar ritual items, or other props might help here, too.

Circles of Concentration

Have you ever watched good ritualists in action? During a rite, notice how they handle all the various tasks – and how they relate to themselves in the space, to the other ritualists, to the attendees, and most importantly, to the Kindreds themselves. And they do this all simultaneously. This skill requires the ritualist to concentrate at various levels, without losing concentration in any single one of them. While this can become automatic for experienced ritualists, it can be difficult to learn at first.

We might call these various levels 'circles' or 'bubbles' of concentration. They require clear focus and energy to be present in order for them to work. Think about the last time you read an engrossing novel, or watched a particularly engaging movie. All of your concentration was centered on that activity, and it would take quite a lot to distract you from your enjoyment of the moment. This is a good example of focus.

Circles of Concentration in the Theatre

In the theatre, a director/teacher named Constantin Stanislawski invented a set of exercises he called the Circles of Concentration or Attention. He would demonstrate it to his class with stage lighting. First, on an otherwise dark stage, a single table would be spotlighted. This was the small circle, which would correspond to the actor himself. After plunging the stage into darkness again, the lights would come up to show a medium circle, with some furniture (including that table) spotlighted. The actor was still at the table, but now had to increase his attention, his focus, over a much larger area. Finally, after another short span of darkness, the lights came up revealing everything on the stage, including the audience seats. This would be the large circle (Stanislavski, 68-89).

Circles of Concentration in Ritual

Now, let's take this idea and adapt it to ritual technique. We have identified four circles of concentration: the ritualist him/herself, the other ritualists in the rite, the attendees, and the Otherworlds. We will explain what we mean in a moment.

Another thing that good focus can give the ritualist is, believe it or not, charisma. Strong focus makes you appear more attractive in some way, and folks have to pay attention.

Kirk likes to tell a story about how this all came together for him:

> Back in the 1980's I attended a drama college in London for a couple of years. I was also an amateur balloonist at the time, and managed to get invited to a reception by the Royal Aero Club, held at the Banqueting House, Whitehall, in honor of a balloonist inventor, Tracy Barnes. The Queen, as President of the Royal Aero Club, would also be attending. Needless to say, I was quite excited.
>
> That same day I learned about the circles of concentration in my acting class. It was a lot to take in, and I worked very hard at it, determined to internalize the technique as quickly as I could. I took this determination with me to the reception.
>
> The center of the hall was roped off, with Girl Guides (British Girl Scouts) 'guarding' the ropes. It was a more innocent time. Early in the reception, after the arrival of the Queen, Prince Philip, and other assorted grandees, the royal party, accompanied by Ladies in

Waiting and all, gathered inside the rope enclosure with the rest of us outside of it. Under normal protocol, the Queen would very slowly walk around the enclosure, talking to a Lady in Waiting, sipping her gin and tonic, while we all watched. I expect that this circumambulation would normally take about half an hour overall. The local British seemed unimpressed (or at least feigned to be so), but I was wide-eyed with wonder.

The Queen started her tour not too far away from me, and was moving slowly, so to keep myself entertained while waiting, I decided to practice creating my circles of concentration. The Queen then stopped right in front of me, and instead of moving on, stayed there for the twenty minutes that I was able to keep the circles going. Prince Philip came over to chat to the Girl Guide next to me, other grandees came over as well, and I was practically in the midst of them all. Then, exhausted, I released my circles - and they all walked away again. Amazing. It was then that I decided that there might be something to these circles after all.

NOTE: The exercises that follow (at least for the 2nd and 3rd circles) need to be done with more than one person. The 1st and 4th circles can be performed alone, but the other two circles are about 'group' ritual as opposed to solitary rites.

1st Circle – The Critic

The 1st Circle is the one that only surrounds you, the ritualist. This layer of focus is designed to keep you aware of yourself, and where you are in space, so that, for instance, you don't trip and fall into the fire. It also is the home of ***The Critic***, you may call it. This is that little voice inside you that tells you when things are wrong (like pointing out the old lady in the back who obviously can't hear you) and that also comments on what you're doing, whether you like it to or not. And often we aren't even aware of our critic.

Some Critics lives at the back of the head, on the right side, and some Critics can live just on your shoulder, like one of those little angels or devils that whispers in your ear. The Critic can be an extremely helpful tool (as when pointing out the deaf old lady) or extremely annoying (as when it points out, unhelpfully, that you obviously screwed up that last invocation). But in any case, don't let your Critic distract you!

Kirk, ever full of stories, has another to relate:

> This is how I discovered and became consciously aware of my personal Critic.
>
> I mentioned earlier that I had been a balloonist. Back in the early 1990's I was also the pilot of a hot-air airship, a sort of pressurized hot-air balloon in the shape of a blimp with a 'car' complete with burners to keep me aloft, and with an engine that ran a propeller behind me for forward thrust. Steering was accomplished by pulling on special ropes designed for that purpose. I had determined that I would try for the world records in distance and duration, and so set off from near our farm in South Dakota in the middle of winter. Cold air would lessen the need for propane fuel for the burners, you see, enabling me to stay aloft longer. Or so I thought.
>
> I flew across the Missouri river (keeping over a bridge nearby just in case something went wrong – I didn't want to land in that icy current) and over Nebraska at about 1000 feet above the ground. Suddenly, a snowstorm developed around me (which the weather folks hadn't foreseen) and the only direction I could see was down. Never mind, I thought, I'll just keep going. In any case, it was solid forest below me, with no obvious landing sites. But then disaster struck when my burners went out and I couldn't get them to relight. While I still had forward motion (thanks to my engine), I no longer had any lift, and so I slowly began to fall out of the sky.
>
> Since I was a flying bomb, with propane tanks dangling everywhere, all connected through a manifold with a series of propane hoses, it was essential that I shut down everything before hitting the ground. Ruptured lines and a spark would be an even worse disaster for me. So I calmly, but quickly, turned all the tanks off, shut down the pilot light, and then managed to steer the

beast towards a hole in the woods that suddenly materialized beneath me. That forward thrust from my engines saved me by enabling me to steer.

Did I just say that I 'calmly' went through my emergency procedures? Well, anyone watching would say that I was calm. But my Critic, at the back of my head, was screaming bloody murder the whole way down to the ground. I was only okay because, for this emergency, I managed to ignore the 'silent' screams.

But my Critic was very much there, and this was the first time I really noticed it and understood what it was.

Exercise 1: Creating the First Circle

Sit quietly in a chair, or stand quietly with your feet planted firmly on the ground, and place your hand over your heart. Feel it beat beneath your hand.

Close your eyes.

In your mind's eye, imagine a bubble of energy come out of your heart and slowly surround you in all directions. The bubble, or circle, is really no bigger than you are.

What does it feel like? Can you see it? What does it look like?

Feel yourself inside of your body. Notice the itch behind your left knee or the feel of your feet inside your shoes. Feel your clothes on your shoulders. Become aware of your entire self.

Now open your eyes, but keep that circle alive - be totally aware of it, and of yourself, while your eyes are open.

Now relax and release your circle. Repeat this exercise a few times until you are sure you have the hang of it.

2nd Circle – The Connection

The 2nd Circle or bubble is all about you and the relationship you will have with the other ritualists in the rite with you. In addition to having a circle that surrounds yourself, you will also need one that surrounds you and your ritual partners. This is because you will occasionally need to relate to them directly, particularly in lore plays, as well as keep track of where they are in relation to you at all times. It really looks dumb when ritualists collide or step on each other's feet, knock over the Well, or accidentally knock ritual offerings out of each other's hands, etc.

In lore plays the people enacting the myth will need to relate to each other like actors on a stage, living in the moment, with clear focus on each other.

I call this circle ***The Connection*** because it is all about connecting with those closest to you in a rite, theatrically speaking. I mean those people you depend upon in order for the rest of the rite to go well.

Now let me be clear that it is necessary for the ritualist to create *both* of these circles simultaneously, and keep them both going for the entire rite. This takes practice, and while it may seem difficult and tiring at first, in time it will become easy and second nature. Remember, practice makes perfect!

Exercise 2: Connecting With Your Partner – The 2nd Circle

Stand facing your partner, and each of you place the palm of your hand on the other person's heart.
a. Breathe together, coming into sync with each other.
b. Feel the other person's heartbeat.
c. Place your other hand on top of your partner's hand on your heart.

Now close your eyes and create your 1st Circle. See it as a bubble only surrounding you, and nothing else. Make it strong and firm.

Then when you are ready,
a. Create a second circle or bubble out from your heart and have it completely enclose both of you (including your 1st Circle bubble).
b. When this new circle is strong and firm, **open your eyes and drop your hands.**

Is your 1st Circle still going strong? Are you still aware of your feet in your shoes, and the feel of your clothes on your shoulders?

Is your 2nd Circle still enclosing both of you? Is your connection to the other person still there?

Now drop both circles and relax. Repeat this exercise a few times until you are sure you have the hang of it.

3rd Circle – Awareness

The 3rd Circle is all about remembering that there are folks here attending your rite. It's all too easy to get all wrapped up in yourself or with your fellow ritualists and lose track of everyone else present. And this can lead to disaster.

A good ritualist will develop eyes in the back of his or her head. They can feel what is going on all over the ritual space whether they can see it or not. They know where the other ritualists are at all times and they can feel the presence of every single attendee in the circle, including those behind them. These ritualists can also sense drops or holes in the energy around them, which often result from attendees being unable to see or hear what is going on. This sense of Awareness can be extremely helpful for the well-trained ritualist. And it can be learned.

Exercise 3: Finding Awareness with the 3rd Circle

Note: This exercise requires a third person to act as a ritual attendee.

Stand with your partner back to back, with your shoulders touching. Grasp your partner's hands and keep your eyes facing forward.

The third person (the attendee) should stand to one side so that neither of the other two is facing him or her directly. The attendee should focus on the other two during this exercise.

With your back to your partner, holding hands and touching shoulders, create your 1st Circle until it is strong and firm.

Now create your 2nd Circle, throwing it around the two of you. As soon as it, too, is strong and firm:

    a.   Let go of each other's hands
    b.   Take one step away from the other person

Are you two still connected? Can you feel the other person standing behind you?

Now create a third circle or bubble out of your heart, and cast it around all three of you *without* looking at the third person. Feel the other two people present - know where they are, sense their breathing.

Repeat this exercise a few times until you are sure you have the hang of it.

Remember, it is necessary for the ritualist to create *all three* of these circles simultaneously, and keep them both going for the entire rite. This takes practice, and while it may seem difficult and tiring at first, in time it will become easy and second nature. Remember, (perfect) practice makes perfect!

4th Circle – Boundaries

So far in this set of exercises we have been concentrating on focus in *this* world. Now we will hold all three circles while opening our hearts and mind's eyes to the Otherworlds as well.

In addition to knowing just where we are in space, and to relating to our fellow ritualists, and to being aware of everyone else in the circle, we also have to be able to embrace and interface with the Otherworlds when we make our invocations to the Kindreds.

And all of this has to be done simultaneously!

While you don't need to have the Gates open to do this exercise, it certainly doesn't hurt. If you can, perform a small rite, open the Gates, and prepare to make offerings to the Kindreds while you practice, below.

Exercise 4: Crossing the Boundary

Note: This exercise is written for three people, but it can also be performed alone. Just do the 1st and 4th Circle sections and you'll be fine.

Option 1 – As in exercise #3, stand with your back to your partner, shoulder to shoulder, holding hands, while the third person (the attendee) stands to the side, focusing on the two of you.

Option 2 – All three of you stand with your backs to each other, making a triangle, shoulder-to-shoulder and holding hands.

Option 3 – If working alone, ignore the 2nd and 3rd Circles below.

Now -

Create your 1st Circle - get it strong and firm.

While holding your 1st Circle:
- Create your 2nd Circle - let go of each other's hands and step away, keeping your connection with each other strong.

While holding your 1st and 2nd Circles:
- Create your 3rd Circle - feel a deep awareness of the third person.

Now, while holding your 1st, 2nd and 3rd Circles:

a. Close your eyes and in your mind's eye see the Gates open as you experience it best. Open your eyes and see light sparkling at the corners of your eyes and movement just out of your vision. Then see, feel and hear the presence of the Cosmos open to you.
b. Keeping all four circles strong and clear make an invocation and offering to a Spirit of your choosing.
c. See the Spirit approach. Hear the breathing of the Spirit as it approaches. Feel the footfall of the Spirit as it approaches.
d. If there are more of you doing the exercise, have each in turn make an invocation. Keep all the Spirits called in your mind's eye - **while also keeping the other three circles strong and clear.**
e. Thank the Spirits, close the Gates, release the Circles and relax.

With practice, these exercises will become natural, and won't require much thought. If you combine these exercises with those elsewhere in this book, you will have what you need to allow inspiration in ritual to flow easily through you, giving you what you need to effectively lead others to the Kindreds.

Being a Leader, Being a Follower

No matter what your role in a ritual, whether you are clergy or lay-person, wedding officiant or ring-bearer, if you are doing work with others then you will find yourself doing two things in every ritual: leading and following.

Leading may be as exciting and prominent as having all eyes on you as you consecrate a new altar or as quiet and seemingly unimportant as singing a chant at the back of the room, but both these are opportunities for leadership in ritual.

Following may be as obvious as repeating words a priestess speaks, or it might be something you wouldn't think of as following, like speaking the "call" part of a call-and-response prayer.

These things might seem counterintuitive, but group ritual is an holistic experience, one where no one controls all aspects and no one is powerless to influence others. Simply being in ritual is an exercise in personal responsibility for the entire process, just as much as it is an exercise in shared responsibility.

Leading in Ritual

First, we'll focus on what it means to lead in ritual. As mentioned, your actions in ritual, even if all you do is observe, is a leadership function.

If you find yourself at a ritual with others and you don't have a part, it is vital that you recognize that your actions *still* affect the way that others experience ritual. If you sit in the back and yawn and shift your weight constantly, you will distract others, or (worse) lead them to do exactly the same thing.

Don't make the mistake of believing that just because you can't be seen, you can't affect the rite! It's entirely possible that all those other senses that everyone has will pick up what you're doing!

If you have a part in the ritual, not matter how big or how small, remember that your performance will bring others to the experience of ritual, to that fire that burns at *your* center. It is incredibly important that you realize both the power *and* the responsibility that this entails.

Here are a few basic points to remember about ritual. It's not really all that hard to lead, but you do need to know a few key things before you start to do it!

- **Always remember: it's not about me.** We like to think that the ritual that we're doing is important, and thus we, who are leading it, are also important. While this is true and we are important, *we are no more important than anyone else participating.* Remember that you're there to provide an experience to others as well as to yourself.

- **Leading means remaining aware of the little things: the "Critic" and the presence of others.** If you're leading the rite or doing a part in ritual, then you need to be aware of things going on. This means different things for different people:
    - **For the head ritualist,** it means that you need to make sure that everything is going as planned: all the parts are being done in order, no one is too close to the fire, and that the pace of the rite is correct.
    - **For someone doing multiple things or leading others** (such as a bard, seer, warrior, etc.), it means that you need to make sure that your parts
    - **For someone with a single part or prayer,** it means being aware of where you are in the ritual, knowing what comes before your part, where everything you need is, and where you are supposed to be. It also helps to know who comes next, especially if you are expected to cue them.
    - **For the participant,** it means that you need to be aware of how you are comporting yourself in ritual so that you are not distracting others, and so that you're aware of things you're supposed to participate in.

- **Leading requires acceptance that you won't always "feel it" like you expect.** This is a harsh truth that people who begin to lead in ritual don't often count on: occasionally (especially the first few times you lead ritual), you won't get the same things out of ritual that you did before you had a part. Even more interesting is that sometimes, you learn just how different it is in public ritual when you stand up in front of others and do something for the first time. The key thing is: it's never the same in public as it is in private, and as you lead ritual, you will find that the experiences you have begin to "settle in" over time, and practice is the only way to make that happen.

Following in Ritual

Now that we've spoken about leading in ritual, let's speak a bit about following.

As mentioned above, everyone follows in ritual, even a person who writes, directs, and stars in a public ritual. Most people experience the "following" aspects of ritual through participation rather than performance, but even ritual leaders must follow each other, the folk, and the crowd of spirits in every ritual.

While a key aspect of following in ritual is being willing to "go along with" the leaders, this should not be confused with blind following. Ritual, particularly modern pagan ritual, requires us to think about where we are going and to actively choose to go to those places, or to quietly and respectfully bow out of the rite if we do not agree to go to those places.

One of the things that ritual leaders have to learn to do is to follow each other. The parts of a ritual cannot be disconnected and disparate, but they need to flow with and into one another, feeding and strengthening each other. Even if you have a part, you need to follow and experience the ritual so that you can be a part of it, rather than trying to control it.

Here are some basic tips for following when you are in ritual:

- **Always remember: it's not about me.** Yes, we said that about leading as well, but here, it's a bit different. Again, it is not only our experience that matters, but the ability to provide that experience to others *as a community*. Seek to understand how your experience can help others achieve a similar experience.

- **"Following" does not mean "giving up" or "being passive."** Just because we don't have an assigned part in the ritual does not mean that we simply *take* from the ritual without *giving back* to it. Help raise energy, focus the work, and sing with the others. Who knows, you might just help someone else get the courage to participate more just by being an active participant!

- **Following is an active, thoughtful action that allows time for consideration and feeling.** This is a key concept for leaders in a rite as well as for individuals who are participating. During the rite, be thoughtful about what you are feeling, but don't be lost in thought. Be aware of what is going on around you, but keep the sense of pace and movement. Use the Circles of Concentration exercise to connect with your fellow ritualists.

Articulating Ritual Vision

Every ritualist who has spent time trying to explain something that sounded "really cool" when they thought it up will know that articulating what you want to have happen in a ritual can be very, very difficult. Often, people have difficulty explaining what they want to have happen to others, and so the end result that appears at a ritual sometimes falls a bit flat (or worse).

So assuming you know what you want to do, and you can see how you want it done, how do you explain this to others?

- **Grow it from something smaller.** If you already do something like it, start by thinking about this new thing as an "improvement" or "small change" to the current process, and explain it using comparative phrases.

- **Draw it or draft it.** You don't have to be a talented artist to use pictures to explain what you'd like to do. You also do not have to be a talented writer to draft stage directions. Visual aids and explanatory scripts can go a long way to explain what you'd like to try.

- **Demonstrate it on a smaller scale.** Don't try to get 20 people to stand in a circle and dance a new dance: teach it to four people and have them help others learn. This is particularly effective with singing, drumming, and other musical or dance pieces (see "shills" later in this book).

- **Never try something new after one explanation just before ritual (*a.k.a.* the "Earth Mother, Blossom Lifter" disaster).** Set up dress rehearsals, sing through new songs at liturgy meetings, and have shills prepared. Three Cranes Grove, ADF, once tried to sing "Earth Mother, Blossom Lifter" in a ritual without rehearsing it. Sure, we had the words and we'd listened to the melody, but it turns out that the song was so difficult that everyone sang it differently. It was not a pretty sound.

Creating a Script

So, you have your ideas in order and you're ready to lead people in a ritual. Now, all we need is a script, right? Because modern Pagans often either create their scripts either by consensus or dictatorship (or somewhere along a general continuum between those), it can lead to personality conflicts if we are unaware of the ways that others do ritual work.

The work of creating and scripting rituals for a group can be done in several ways, but they fall into general categories, based on whether the individuals have a desire to control the rite, or to provide vision for others to work with.

Hope For the Best types tend to have little in the way of an overarching vision for the rite and little taste for controlling the function of rituals.

Controller types have a strong vision for a rite and a desire to make the rite go the way they envision it by controlling the details.

Laissez-Fair types tend to have a strong desire to control their own part, but little concern for the overall flow of the rite.

Gentle Hand types like to focus more on the overall vision than on details, leading them to be less concerned with how people create parts and more concerned that the vision is consistent.

As mentioned, these are general categories. Because they move along two axes (vision and control of detail), you can visualize their relationships in quadrants:

More Visionary

The Laissez-Fair	The Controller
The Hope for the Best	The Gentle Hand

More Controlling ↑

So, as a person becomes more visionary, they move to the right, and as a person becomes more controlling, they move up. People will occasionally move from place to place in the quadrants, depending on the rite they are working on: a festival rite might bring out different characteristics in someone than a rite of passage, for instance.

None of these positions should be considered "better than" any of the others; they are merely different ways to experience and interact with others in ritual. Knowing where you fall and where others fall within these quadrants can help you reduce conflict and work together as you prepare for rituals as a group.

One thing that you may notice very quickly is that quadrants across from each other tend to fit well together: a Gentle Hand can lend vision to a Laissez-Fair and build a spectacular ritual team, while a Controller can provide direction and vision to a Hope For the Best and both will find a very deep ritual experience.

On the other hand, quadrants directly adjacent to one another often have issues working together: Controllers and Gentle Hands clash on questions of vision, and Hope For the Bests frustrate the Laissez-Fair in questions of control.

So, here's a quick field guide to identifying each type (among both ritual leaders and ritual participants, because both fall into these categories!) so that you can start with some perspective about how you might work with others.

The Controller:

Leaders who fit in this quadrant are often easy to spot: typically, they like one person (often themselves) or a very small team to write the script and provides it to others. This sort of person is often in danger of "falling into a rut" and repeating the same rite year after year, or even putting things that worked in one ritual into another rite where they might not work so well.

Participants who fit here usually wish to write their own parts, and they often become upset if they do not have something to "make their own." They will typically ask for specific parts (often the same part each time). They will also often take the initiative and offer to write parts for others, as well.

Occasionally, when leaders and participants of this type have small disagreements about either the details or the overall vision of the rite, very large interpersonal explosions can result, but this sort of ritualist is just as likely to keep it all inside, secure in the knowledge that they're "right" anyway.

Another thing that seems counterintuitive is that people who insist on always doing things "off the cuff" can often fall into this category (most people think they would fall into the "Hope For the Best" category): having no style of your own is just as much a detail- and vision-oriented focus as refining that style over time.

The Laissez-Fair:

Laissez-Fair comes from the French for "hands off." Leaders who fit into this quadrant tend to be just that regarding the details: most often, everyone writes their own part and turns it in for assembly before the rite, and the leader is unlikely to seek a unified vision for the whole rite, though they will often provide exact instructions. In other words, it is the strict details that are important, not the story that they tell. This style works very well for technical ritual work, such as high ceremonial magic.

Participants who fit into this quadrant are also very "hands off," but in a different way: they want to write their own parts without input from the ritual leader, and they may be "touchy" about their parts if they are very controlling. Typically, they are less concerned about the overall "look and feel" of the rite, and more concerned with their own parts.

Leaders and participants of this type can also be very defensive of their work, and they will often hold things in for a long time, only to explode if someone questions their work. This comes from a feeling that if someone didn't like something, then they don't like the ritualist. This is because a Laissez-Fair type identifies very strongly with the ideas that they have and the details they have built, so in their mind questioning the idea is also questioning the person who had the idea.

The Gentle Hand:

Leaders who fit into this quadrant will often have a very solid (often even a specific) vision for the rite, but is usually very comfortable with others taking control of their parts. Typically, one person, or a team (Gentle Hands like teams), will review and help each person write their part. Often, however, this help is less technical, and more broad-based: Gentle Hands are less likely to provide detail help, and more likely to say, "I like this, but our theme is X, and you're talking about Y." They rarely tell you how to get from "Y" back to "X."

Participants in this quadrant prefer to receive minimal guidance and let inspiration take them in the rite. They often want general information about the rite so they can work with it rather than specific instructions about what to do (they can be insulted if you get too specific). When the time comes to ask about how the rite went, they tend to provide feedback about their vision for their part, but not on the rite as a whole.

Gentle Hands like to have a very light touch on the work of others, and to have only a light touch on their parts. They are also prone to flights of fancy, however: by focusing on the broad vision, they often fail to provide enough detail for others to build their parts, which can be quite frustrating, and the Gentle Hands can be annoyed by continual requests for more detail. Occasionally, they will also forget some of the key details to keeping a rite moving smoothly, which can lead to a lot of friction among ritual teams.

The Hope For The Best:

Leaders who fit into this quadrant often expect their co-ritualists to write their own parts, though they often don't ask to see them until after the rite (if at all). It is very common for these individuals to not have their own work scripted, either because they have enough experience leading ritual to do this, or because they have a lot of confidence in their own ability (rightly placed or not).

Participants who fit in this quadrant prefer to do one of three things: do what they have always done, use a pre-written part, or to make it up on the spot. This type is the most likely to use a script in ritual (though they're not the only ones who do).

A quick word on "doing what they've always done," which is also a characteristic of Controller participants: the motivations are different for Hope For the Best participants than they are for Controllers. Typically, while the Controller wants the same part because they know the details inside and out and they can do it "correctly" in their eyes, the Hope For the Best wants the same part because they don't feel comfortable with any other part.

Leaders and participants in this category enjoy relaxed ritual that doesn't have a lot of detail. They can often become frustrated with attempts to gently guide them toward a greater vision, as well as attempts to force a change in their work, because they need both the detail and the vision to be comfortable with what they're doing. This group is the least likely to have an emotional outburst regarding their work, but you will notice when they leave your ritual working group because this sort of person is incredibly valuable in that they can work with nearly everyone, so long as they feel respected.

Hope For the Best folks may seem like a group that no one wants to be in: they're the "lowest" quadrant on the scale, but in many cases, some of our best ritualists in the modern Pagan movement fall into this category: often, they just love to be included, and they have a skill level that lets them "wing it" with at least as much skill as those who spend hours preparing their parts. Still, they got to that place through practice and dedication, not through "winging it" from the start.

Exercise: Placing Yourself, Placing Others

Place yourself on this chart, then place a couple of other people you have worked with. Then, ask them to place you on the same chart (without telling them where you think you fall), and see if you fall where you think you do!

More Visionary →

	The Laissez Fair	The Controller
↑ More Controlling		
	The Hope for the Best	The Gentle Hand

Understanding Space

The space you have ritual in can be simple or elaborate, but one constant is that when you do public ritual, you will have *people* in it. The question of space, then is less about "how will I deal with the space for ritual?" and more, "How will I deal with the people in that space?" Fortunately, the theatre has answered most of those questions for us!

Theatre and ritual are, as you have already noticed, intimately linked. The same configurations that theatre uses are the ones available to us as ritualists, so we need to pay attention to how they are dealt with in that world, to understand how they can be dealt with in our world.

The three arrangements we will discuss are **proscenium**, **thrust**, and **arena**. Two others, sometimes called "cabaret" (where the audience sits on two adjoining sides) and "stadium" or "alley" (where the seats are on either side of the stage, such as on the east and west sides, and actors/ritualists can move off-stage on the north and south sides) provide the same challenges and benefits as thrust and arena, respectfully, so we won't cover them here.

Proscenium

Proscenium arrangements are designed to provide "windows" into the action on the stage: the audience is therefore "outside" the action, looking in. The entire action takes place within the forward view of the audience member, and the audience is "in it together," meaning that they are all observing the same thing with the same backdrop. Additionally, there are places outside the view of the audience: the areas backstage and in the wings that are generally obscured from the audience's view, either via curtains or scenery. (Figure 1, right)

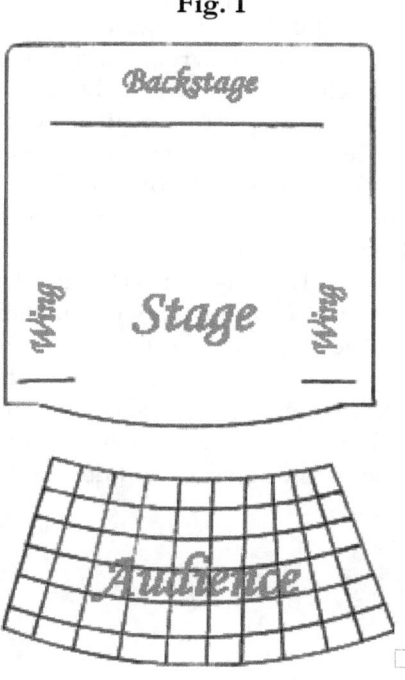

Fig. 1

Proscenium theatre arrangement, drawn by Rev. Michael J Dangler

Major advantages provided by this configuration include a high level of control over what is seen and heard by the attendees; the ability to have a "backstage area" where people can prepare to do roles or set up and store props; a definite clarity of roles (everyone knows who is a "performer" and who is an audience member); and it is highly scalable, allowing to no set upward limit (excepting space and sound projection limits) to attendance.

Because this is the way we watch most theatre plays (and all movies), this type of arrangement leads to a few particular disadvantages. The first major disadvantage is a definite "performance" feeling for those watching: audience participation is minimized in this type of configuration. Mainstream churches (particularly mega-churches) are set up in this format most often: it is by far the most effective way of providing ritual to large numbers of people all at once. Still another disadvantage is that there are often issues with "line of sight" and the creation of "bad seats" where a person in a particular seat may not be able to see everything that is happening.

The primary disadvantage that a Grove will encounter is the "church-like" feel of this configuration. The primary way to avoid this is not to engage this configuration until the limitations of the "thrust" configuration are overwhelming the disadvantages of the proscenium configuration. Engaging the congregation in roles and direct participation are also good ways to reduce the "church-like" feel.

Line-of-sight issues and bad seats can be minimized by keeping visual obstacles to a minimum, and increasing the apron of the stage to give the arrangement more thrust. Also, using ritual spaces already designed for this style of performance (rather than attempting this without a stage or a rise to the seats) can also help minimize these issues. Ensuring that the performers project toward the audience and do not turn their back on them is also vital.

Thrust

The term "thrust" comes from the notion that this configuration "thrusts" the actor into the audience: it can be generally described as a configuration where the audience is arranged around the stage, which is usually completely visible except from behind (or nearly behind). (Figure 2, right)

The primary advantages of this configuration include a more intimate feel (the audience feels more a part of what is going on, partially because the

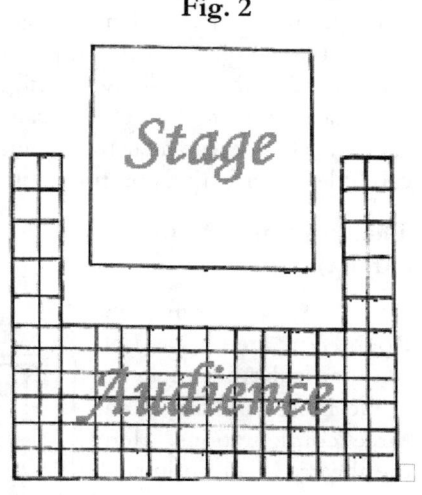

Thrust theatre arrangement, drawn by Rev. Michael J Dangler

audience is also in their field of vision: either across from them or to their side). Additionally, this configuration reduces barriers: there are no wings to the stage, and there are rarely curtains or other visual blocks, meaning that prop and setting changes are rarer. Because the audience is so close to the actors, there is less of a "performance" feel to rituals in this configuration, and it feels less like "church" to most attendees, because it does not match the experiences they had of church growing up.

The primary disadvantages include reduced projection options: in this configuration, the speaker will be in profile to (or turned away from entirely) at least half the audience at any given time. In addition, because there is less access to off-stage area, changing the setup of the ritual area is more complicated, and there is a smaller staging area for the next speaker to prepare in. Altars and props must have greater dimensionality (they must be "presentable" from several other directions, rather than just in a "straight-on" view) since the audience can now see at least three sides of any object.

Mitigating these disadvantages is generally not too complicated: by training ritualists where to project their voice to (and to teach them to treat all areas of the audience the same), the projection issues can be reduced. For particularly large groups, microphones and amplifiers can go a long way. Storage of props can be best mitigated through preparation: either placing them in the charge of the ritualist who will use them, or finding space on the altar. Longer altar cloths can hide many imperfections in setup (such as cheap altar tables) and flowers or other decorations can hide imperfections on props until they are needed.

Theatre-in-the-Round (Arena)

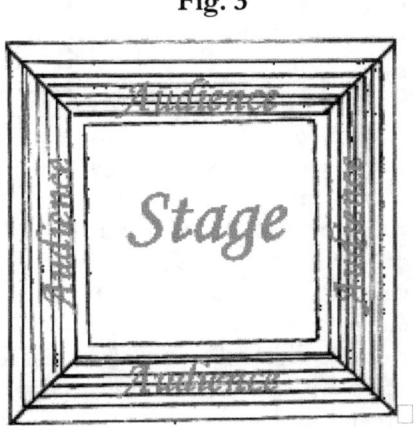

Fig. 3

Arena theatre arrangement, drawn by Rev. Michael J Dangler

Theatre in the Round (or Arena) has only one particular advantage: it is the most intimate of the three configurations. Here, the theatre is set up in such a way as to have the audience on all sides of the stage, usually in bleacher-style seating. (Figure 3 at right)

This configuration works only in very small groups (roughly no more than 9-13 in our experience) and is best suited for rituals where parts are chosen at random and on the spot (e.g. going around a circle and doing the next part as it comes up rather than assigning the parts in advance). For rituals of this size, where the participants truly are comfortable being intimate, the disadvantages are negated by the small number of attendees.

Those disadvantages begin to quickly rear their head as soon as you exceed the upper limits of the round configuration, however. This form of theatre configuration places extreme limits on projection: no matter what you do, you will always have roughly half the audience to your back, or out of your line of sight. This means that no matter what you do to project, at least half the people there will not hear what you have to say.

Additionally, there is no prop storage, meaning that you cannot place anything outside of the sight of the ritual attendees, because someone will have a view of it.

If forced to work in an arena configuration, the best thing to do is to turn it into a thrust if at all possible. That means moving the altar to one end of the ritual space and placing all celebrants at that end as well. Doing this can keep the intimate feel of the circle for most participants, and the "wall of celebrants" can remain behind the speaker and form the "backstage" area where there is no audience. While this leaves the celebrants out of the rite as participants, it creates a better experience for everyone else in attendance, who can now hear and see everything you are doing.

Exercise: Placing the Altar, Facing the Folk

Look around the room you are in, or go outside and find a space you would like to do a group ritual. Think about where you would put the fire, your working table, and any other ritual tools you might need. Where would you ask the folk to stand? Where would you stand, as leader, and where would you put your other ritual actors? If you had 6 people show up, how would you configure all these things? What if you had 20 people show up? 70?

Think about venues available to you that seat over 100 people. How would you set one of those up for a ritual?

Key questions to think about in each situation:

1. How would I distribute the Waters of Life or Cakes and Ale to that many people?
2. What about all the "stuff" I brought with me that isn't a specifically ritual item (such as boxes or tubs that might be used to carry ritual supplies)?
3. How would people approach the altar? At what point does it get too hard for your ritual participants (people who have parts) to reach the altar efficiently? How can you mitigate those issues?

4. Can everyone see everything you do, or do you need to make things bigger to accommodate people in the "cheap seats?" How can you make sure that there are as few "cheap seats" as possible?

Additional Work

The rough stuff is done: now, what can you do to make any ritual go a bit smoother? Improvisation is something we all must do, whether we like it or not. Music adds an amazing new dimension to ritual that cannot be described until it is felt. Meditation and trance work deepen the experience for everyone involved. Ritual critique is a harsh, but very necessary, lesson that we all must work with.

This chapter will help you work through these topics and apply them in your practice, both public and private.

Memorization

When folks first start out, doing ritual in public can be quite intimidating; memorizing scripts adds even more pressure to the mix. We may think that we have memorized something, but when we get up there, in front of all those people, the words just fly out of our heads. As a result, we see scripts in a lot of rites.

Now, reading from scripts is not necessarily a bad thing. It's a wonderful way to get a group of people together and do effective ritual while learning how it's done. As Chief Liturgist for Sonoran Sunrise Grove, Kirk used elaborate scripts for the first few years while their liturgy gelled, and as a result most members internalized the words and prayers quite well. Well enough, in fact, to eventually lose the scripts altogether and start improvising with all that had been learned.

An argument can be made about perfection in ritual – the ancient Romans and Vedics were insistent on rites being done perfectly. In Rome a ritual had to be started over if even the slightest mistake was made: this outlook on ritual makes scripts very attractive!

However, there are down sides to reading scripts in ritual. For one thing, the celebrant is looking down at a piece of paper instead of out into the world, where they can connect with the attendees and 'see' the Powers in the Otherworlds. Scripts get dropped and people lose their places. It is also difficult to keep up the pace and flow of a rite when the celebrants are concentrating on their scripts instead of on the rite itself. ("Is it my turn yet?" or "Where are we? I'm lost.") Now, having said that, it is certainly possible to have wonderful rituals when reading from scripts. It's just very, very difficult and requires enormous preparation. In the theatre they give whole workshops to actors on how to read from scripts during auditions. We aren't able to do that.

Memorization Tips

There are probably as many ways to memorize something as there are people doing the memorization. One method you can use is repetition, backed up with coffee.

Caffeine is a stimulant and well known to aid in memorization. Hollywood and the theatre run on caffeine. If you can't take caffeine (and not everyone can) then you'll have to go without. But it should still be possible to memorize things.

Also, speak your words 'out loud' when memorizing text. And eventually do so in full voice. There is a truism in the theatre that applies here,

"You cannot do what you have not rehearsed."

Exercise: Simple Memorization

a. Take a poem or prose piece that has at least 15-20 lines of text to learn. Pick a time of day that you will be able to work on this daily over a three or four-day period. You want to work on learning your piece everyday for a while. This is important.

b. Say the first line over and over a few times **out loud** until you can say the entire line on your own without looking at the text.

c. Do the same with the second line, until you can say all of it without looking at the text.

a. Now say the first and second lines over and over until you can say both of them without looking.

b. Add a third line to your repetition and when you are able, add it to the first two lines.

c. Continue with this until you can recite the entire poem (or until your head explodes).

d. Once you get this far, STOP for today. Tomorrow, you may find that you can't remember 'any' of the poem. That's normal. Just start over from the beginning and try again.

e. After a few days of this, the poem will become memorized.

f. To internalize the poem, recite it at odd times and in different situations, like when out for a walk, or driving the car, or grocery shopping. Reciting the piece when distracted will help push it into your internalized memory.

Variation

Some folks like to start with the 'last' line of the poem or prose piece, and work backwards. This can be good because the end of the piece becomes firmly lodged in your brain, and it's the end of the piece that can give folks the most trouble.

Some folks like to speak their lines in a bathroom, where the sound reverberates and sounds cool – it helps them remember. Others like to learn their lines in different orders, like starting at the beginning, then starting at the end, then starting at the middle. What works for you is what works for you.

TIP – **Don't use a mirror!** Learning or practicing your lines in front of a mirror can be a bad thing. You end up associating certain lines and actions with your own facial expressions, etc., and when you get into ritual and don't have a mirror to gaze into, you may discover that you can't remember anything.

TIP – **Rhyme and meter are easier to memorize than prose.** While this isn't true for everyone, it's true for most people. The rhyme and/or the meter will help to lodge the words, in the correct order, in your head. It's much like learning your favorite songs (though songs also have a tune to hang on to, making them easier still).

Improvisation

No matter how well we script our rituals, something will always go in a manner that is unexpected. Improvisation is the intersection of intuition and technical knowledge: it is inspiration at its finest, the fire of poets.

Keys to Improvising Well

Spend time learning and researching: memorize common patterns, texts, phrases, and other structures. The process of memorizing texts, learning ritual phrases, and the structures of both ritual and myth will be vitally important when you go off-script the first time, whether it is intentional or not.

It often sounds weird to speak of memorization and improvisation in the same breath: we tend to think about improvisation as free-flowing, unbound by structure or convention, and maybe even funny. What we don't see in improvisational comedy or drama is that the actors have certain structures and rules that they are following at all times. These rules can be bent (and occasionally broken) to great effect, but it is an awareness of the rules of the game, as well as the language of that game, that really makes the improvisation *work*.

Memorize key points you want to make: for most rites, this is approximately three different points per prayer. The most common reason that people freeze when speaking is that they have lost their "map" of the conversation, and they are unsure where to go next. If you know what three points you want to make, you can simply move on to the next point if you forget where you are in a prayer.

Remember, you already have the language you will need available because you have been reading the lore, learning the common ritual phrases, and picking up patterns that your group normally uses. If you know the three points you want to make, you will have no trouble adding a flourish or two to the points to make it sound like you didn't lose your place at all.

Bookends are a sub-set of memorizing key points: if you have a set few lines that you use to begin and end every prayer, you will find that you can both begin and end strong. Most people only remember the beginning and end of any spoken performance, anyway, so having these memorized will allow you to bring flow back to the rite even if you got lost somewhere in the middle.

Remain aware of others: what they do, say, and the tone of their work should reflect your actions, words, and tone! You cannot and should not be the only actor on the stage.

If the person who spoke before you in the rite was speaking fast because they were nervous, and you know that the person after you has a very serious piece that will be spoken slowly, it is your job to correct the tempo of the rite and bridge the two pieces.

You also need to match the gestures and movements of others in the rite. If you are honoring the fire after another person honors the well, and that person goes to the well and makes a dramatic gesture toward it, you should do something similar with the fire. (Though remember the rules of intentional movement!)

Ensure that you are prepared for your part and that you know when you go. If there is a person who is in charge of the rite wait patiently for the cue before you start to speak (sometimes, a priest may need to change the order of things on the fly, and might not be able to get a message to you that things changed before it is "your turn"). If there is no single person in charge, then make sure that you're ready as soon as the person who went before you finishes.

The most important thing to remember is that improvisation is not, despite what you may see in improv comedy troops, about being funny, light-hearted, or free-flowing. There is structure to improvisation, though that structure may be difficult for someone outside to see.

117

Using Music Effectively in Ritual Space

The role of the Bard is one that is often given to the grove member with the most musical interest. Unfortunately, interest doesn't necessarily equal experience, and even with experience in music, not many folks have experience using music for more than entertainment purposes. So, where does one start when asked to incorporate music in ritual?

There are several key places where music can be an effective tool, particularly chants that include the entire congregation. From the very beginning, music will start the work of creating one of the most important elements of ritual, the "group mind," by getting everyone involved in the same activity. This will also serve to create the deeper, individual "ritual mind" as folks continue to chant and allow their minds to begin the process of dissociating and leaving behind the worries of their busy lives.

Once the group mind is established and liminality sets in, the remaining songs are centered on maintaining this phenomenon so that the energy will continue to build as the rite progresses. The easiest way to do that is through attention to the ritual choreography. Look at the liturgy and try to visualize what will be happening. Are there places in the rite where the folk will have a lapse in time between parts such as an open offering time for people to come forward with individual offerings? Is the ritual team moving around without dialogue? Does something on the altar need to be rearranged for a purpose mid-rite? Is there a change in setting for the working? All of these things can be very draining on the power built during a rite because they hold potential for the folk to disengage and fall back into mundane-world conversation causing the group mind to dissolve. When this happens, you will lose energy that may be needed later in the rite.

The two main areas that are commonplace culprits for energy drain are during the individual praise offerings and during the sharing of the Blessings. If the energy wanes during the individual praise offerings, the Final Sacrifice will not be as great. If the energy wanes during the Blessings, the energy flow coming back to us will begin to ground out and there will be less energy available for performing the Workings. The addition of a chant or even just drums in these places will make a big difference in the effectiveness of your rites.

A key question that new ritual leaders ask is, "How do I begin introducing musical pieces?" Groves and solitaries who are not used to music will probably not enjoy a rite that all of a sudden contains six songs! The best thing to do is to begin by plugging in the Portal Song for the (re)creation of the Cosmos. Not only does this do the work of the group mind, but it also channels energy into the magical work of rearranging the cosmos to your align at your Sacred Center. Further, since the Portal Song is so common among ADF groves and festivals, in general, it will help when/if you travel to connect with the other ADF members. As one Three Cranes member once said, "If ADF has an anthem, it's the Portal Song."

From there, start small. Add in a processional, some simple chant that you can repeat a few times. You may wish to encourage someone to bring a drum and work up to music with words over time. Also, lack of a musician is no reason to feel as though this technique will not work for you. There is no harm in recorded music, and you may find that singing along with a recording helps the folk let go even more, because they often do not feel as exposed. After all, one of the main reasons people do not include musical pieces is lack of self-confidence in musical ability.

Remember, the purpose of any rite is to create and maintain that liminal space, that misty space between the worlds in which to do the work of Our Druidry and honor the Kindred. If the folk have no idea what time it is or how long you've been in ritual space at the end of the rite, then your job was well done!

The following outline is a simple tool to aid you in adding music to your rites:

The ADF Core Order of Ritual

1. Initiating the Rite
   - **Add a processional song to create a group mind**
2. Purification - This must take place prior to Opening the Gates
3. Honoring the Earth Mother
4. Statement of Purpose
5. (Re)Creating the Cosmos

- **Consider using the "Portal Song" at this point**
6. Opening the Gate(s) - Must include a Gatekeeper
7. Inviting the Three Kindreds
   - **Add a song here to help keep the folk engaged during any individual offerings**
8. Key Offerings
   - **If you do a second set of praise offerings, another song fits well here**
9. Prayer of Sacrifice
   - **A short chant can be added here for a final raising of energy to help transport the gifts to the Kindreds**
10. Omen
11. Calling (asking) for the Blessings
12. Hallowing the Blessing
    - **After the Waters of life have been announced, music will help keep the folk from disengaging from the ritual mind. This is particularly important if there are workings to take place after the Waters.**
13. Affirmation of the Blessing
14. Workings
    - **Energy might be raised using vocalizations for the purpose of performing a magical act (See below)**
15. Thanking the Beings
16. Closing the Gate(s)
17. Thanking the Earth Mother
18. Closing the Rite
    - **A recessional piece can allow the folks to expel the last bit of excess energy that they have gathered during the rite. This is particularly helpful if there is an intense working.**

Three Tips for Priests Who Can't Sing

1. You do not have to be the lead in every part of the ritual. If you don't have a formally appointed Bard, you may wish to ask for volunteers. You may be surprised at who jumps at the chance when asked a direct question. Your

Bard can be your best ally in ritual space. The Role of a Bard is not too different from that of Lead Liturgist, because the Bard needs to know what is coming next at all times.

2. In the absence of a Bard, choose songs that you know well, and practice singing along with a recording. There are many on the ADF website at http://www.adf.org/rituals/chants

   a. Sing loud enough to keep the air moving through your vocal chords consistently.

   b. Drop your chin. It's common to want to sing to the sky, but that will strain your vocal chords and cause your notes to go off-key.

   c. Both of these things will keep your voice in better tune and help you to project so others can hear you, and if they are merciful, they will sing along.

3. When all else fails, there is no harm in singing along to a recording. The power is in the doing, and it does not matter if the anchor is live or electronic. The energy will move if you can get the folk to join in.

Ending Prayers and Chants in Unison

As stated above, the group mind is crucial to the work of Our Druidry, so we make many efforts to maintain it and deepen it throughout. Regardless of the avenue, the best way to establish, deepen and maintain group mind is to have the folk actually participate in what you are doing. It is helpful to add songs to the rite, true, but some parts of the rite do not lend themselves to song. In fact, during some workings and prayer portions, inserting a song may actually take away from what the liturgy is attempting to do. In addition, adding several songs to a ritual will make it long, long, long—and may do more harm than good if the folk in your area are not used to music.

So, what do you do? Building a common structure, such as what the Cranes call "bookending" our prayers, and keeping the folk well informed will not only achieve this goal, but also deepen ritual experiences. When the folk are more engaged and know what to expect, when you have built anticipations and then fulfilled them, the confidence and comfort borne from familiarity will take liturgy off the paper and translate it into actions pleasing to both the Gods and the folk.

Shills: A Bard's Best Friend(s)

"Shills" are individuals who know what to do, when to do it, and how to do it, so that others will follow their lead and help everyone along. In religious settings, this term is unfortunately most commonly applied to people who "fake" a faith healing so that others will believe, but the term is not, by nature, negative.

Because you cannot spend all your time telling people what actions to do, shills are often the best short-cut to providing instruction without actually telling people how to do every little thing. In other words, shills will help the folk learn by example.

Three Tips for using Shills

- Spread out your singers and individuals skilled in call-and-response
    o Having your singers spread out allows them to see each other and also to encourage others to sing. Often, people will not sing because they are embarrassed, but the presence of someone who knows the words will often encourage them to sing (sometimes softly, sometimes loudly) as part of the group.
- Place your drummers together and closest to the Bard/Lead Druid
    o Because sound does not travel as fast as light, drummers have a tendency to get off-beat if they are more than a few yards apart. Having drummers spread around a circle can lead to disaster in terms of drumming in unison.
- Coordinate any signals you have in advance
    o This is especially important if the priest does not know common musical signals for "stretch it

out" or "stop playing soon." It is also important if you are doing a very focused working, quiet trance, or very loud chant.

Getting People to Participate

So, now that everything is on paper and some key folks have been scattered throughout the folk, all you need to do is execute. If you look comfortable, and if your shills look comfortable, the other people are more likely to be drawn into participating. People who are sure of themselves are far more likely to try something new, so never underestimate the power of a good pre-ritual briefing and a well-organized hand-out.

Preparing For the Unexpected

So here you are, ready for a great rite, and then something goes dreadfully wrong. Perhaps your usual ritual site in the park is flooded, perhaps the skies open and the Thunder Gods drop buckets of rain on your heads, perhaps no one shows up for your rite. What to do?

You have to be able to handle these situations, because they could easily happen to you. The easiest one to deal with is when no one shows up. As disheartening as this can be, piety demands that you perform the rite anyway – after all, it's about honoring the Kindreds, is it not? To walk away and do nothing would be like a slap in the face for Them. Fill your heart with joy and wonder and have a great rite anyway.

The other situations will demand concrete action, and we can't tell you what to do here. My best advice would be to know your ritual area well and always have a back-up plan ready, should one be needed. At least think about all the possible disasters and decide, in advance, what could be done. And then forget about it! Let it go. Should you need to make sudden or drastic changes at the last minute, the possible solutions will fill your mind. You won't need to go looking for them.

Disasters During the Rite

Sometimes, even with the most rehearsed or tightly scripted rite, something dreadful may go wrong. Since it's almost impossible to plan for such things, you may have to 'wing it' and put things right. There are three main things to remember in such a situation:

1) Acknowledge the disaster
2) Use humor to soften it
3) Forget about it and go on

There is a story that Kirk loves to tell about something that happened to him. He relates:

> Once, at a non-ADF festival, it was my job to ordain a new ADF priest in the middle of a full ADF rite I was leading. It was also my job to open the Gates to the Otherworlds, and I decided to do this in my usual manner, spinning in place while holding out a staff to 'stir' the cosmos, chanting the charm, and magically get those gates open.
>
> However, this was a site I was not used to, and it was slightly sloped. It was also as dark as the inside of a cow, and the staff I had borrowed was very top heavy.
>
> So as I was spinning, I suddenly realized that I had lost control and was spinning wildly. Before I could stop myself I knocked over the World Tree (a large branch we had stuck into the ground). In fact, I didn't so much knock it over as send it flying high into the air.
>
> Everyone present froze and held their breath in horror (and amusement, I suspect).
>
> I managed to come to a stop and ended the charm with a shouted, "Let the Gates be open, even if I did knock over the f---ing Tree!"
>
> Everyone laughed and the incident was over. I then proceeded to run the rite as though nothing had happened, and later many of the attendees congratulated me on a powerful and moving ritual.

We have to acknowledge our obvious mistakes because if we don't, the attendees will continue to wonder if it was done on purpose, or if it was really a mistake, or what, and this will pull them out of the rite, distracting their attention.

Humor is helpful in any rite (within limits – don't spoil the magic or intent with too much humor) but in this situation humor is important because it helps to release the tension that suddenly filled everyone at the time of the mishap.

Once the incident is acknowledged and the tension released, it is very, very important to continue with the rite as if nothing had happened. This will re-gather the magic and intent and take everyone back to the business at hand. Only in this way will the incident no longer be a distraction, allowing the rest of the rite to be a success.

Meditation for Groups

Meditation in a group setting is primarily designed to help people *understand* and/or *feel* in similar ways. It builds connections between the folk and helps to draw people together for the rite ahead.

Trancework for Groups

A key thing to remember when doing trancework with groups of people is that not everyone responds the same way to the same images. Some people are more apt to engage with visual descriptions, while others will hear things in trance but cannot see anything. You should always focus on the sense of sight, hearing, and touch, but work on all senses (taste and smell), even if it's only a passing mention.

It is very important to repeat images throughout the meditation: by providing "touchstones" throughout the trance, you will bring them back to the same place, which will keep them from having a different experience than the one you intend.

If you can, start in a familiar or common starting point for each ritual. The best thing to do is to develop an "inner locale" that is shared by everyone in the group, such as a certain grove of trees, or a well, or a cave everyone knows.

Finally, make sure that the place you are doing the meditation or trancework is quiet and private enough that you will not be disturbed.

Once you are ready to start scripting the journey that you will take the group on, you will need to pay attention to a couple of particular tricks that can help everyone move quickly into trance. Start with concrete things:

- The most concrete thing you can have people do is "watch their breath." Breathing is a natural and simple place to start.
    - "For a moment, watch your breath. Breathe in, and out. In, and out..."
- Now that they are aware of this concrete thing, it is time to get a bit more abstract. You will use this pattern:

concrete thing, abstract thing; concrete thing, abstract thing; through the trancework. Ask the participants to feel the weight of the body or the earth supporting them:
    - "Sit quietly, settled upon the earth. Feel gravity pull you down, feel the earth hold you up…"
- You can also have them focus their vision on a flame, well, or other physical thing and use that as the slightly more abstract thing to focus on:
    - "Before you is the flame we have kindled: feel its warmth on your face, see its brightness in your eyes…"
- White noise is another good thing to focus on, especially in louder environments. Drumming or a constant tone also works well for this:
    - "Hear the static of the noise, and let it begin to block out other sounds. Listen to its consistency and chaos…"
- Now, again, move on to less concrete things that are non-specific:
    - Formless mists (if people have closed their eyes)
        - "In your mind's eye, see the mist roll in…"
    - Shapes arising in their focus (if focused on something)
        - "In the focus before you, see the shapes within the flame…"
    - Random but directed ambient noise (if using white noise)
        - "In the chaos of the noise, seek patterns that arise and dissipate…"
- Return to concrete things, then take off toward the goal:
    - "Now, remember your breath, and see the mist part…"

- "Now, see the flames that surround these shapes, and know that they form the salamander's body…"
- "Now, with the pattern in the chaos, seek sounds you understand…"

When you go to bring people out, you will do just the opposite: ask them to see something more abstract, and then slightly more concrete. You can bring them back to the visual or auditory aid, then have them focus on their breathing again, and finally have them wiggle their fingers and toes to get all the way "back in."

It is often good to have a meal after trancework, as food also helps people who have a rough time "coming back" to settle into their bodies.

Ritual Criticism and Review

Ritual criticism can be very hard to start doing, and even harder to keep doing once you've started. It is, however, a vital thing for all modern Pagans to do for every ritual that they perform, especially the public ones. After all, you can bet that even if you don't review and criticize your own ritual work, someone else who attended the rite is almost certainly doing just that!

First: **Review all rites!** Think about what went right, what went wrong, and what mistakes you made (including the ones that were really, really cool). Do not get complacent and avoid critique for any ritual, under any circumstance, even if it is only you reviewing it.

Next, **Consider ritual criticism to only be about the rite!** Never criticize the person who performs it (this does not mean that you can't criticize the way they did things). Remember these two things when working through ritual criticism, whether giving or receiving your criticism:

- **Provide honest feedback that is supportive:** do not be "so honest it hurts," but provide feedback that is genuine but gentle. Understand why you are providing the feedback before you provide it.

- **Accept honest feedback as positively intentioned:** always assume that feedback comes from a place of love (both for you and the Kindreds) rather than a place of intentional "hurt."

Finally, **Do not depend solely on the omens for guidance!** Remember that there are two parties in every rite; those who are honored, and those who do the honoring. Paganism is about reciprocity, so ensure that the concept of *Ghosti* carries through, and that all your rituals are good for the Kindreds as well as the Folk.

Infelicitous Performance

An "infelicitous performance" is any performance that goes "wrong" for some reason. This is after Ronald Grimes' definition (after J.L. Austin), which can be found in his book, *Ritual Criticism* (see "Further Reading"). These can be actions that are invalid (either because they are not allowed by the "rules" of religion or they are simply "wrong"), ineffectual, demeaning or defeatist, or even abusive (defined as "hollow" ritual actions).

It is difficult to talk about how rituals have gone "wrong" without discussing them in very black-and-white terms: most often, we believe that the entire ritual must be void if one thing was done wrong, or we have difficulty discussing a single thing that might have not worked without implying that the entire rite was a failure. By classifying the performance of certain *acts* as infelicitous, we can start to focus on what the real issue is.

Grimes provides a very helpful chart of the terms one might use to discuss the infelicitous nature of the performance of certain acts. We have included it here (slightly altered; we tend to believe that Pagans have a different set of ritual issues than most religions, so we have placed them in what we consider a more logical order).

A Vocabulary for Infelicitous Ritual Performance

1. "Misfire" – Act purported but invalid
    A. "Misinvocation" – Act disallowed
        i. "Non-Play" – Lack of process, or the action is "outside the rules" and "breaks" the ritual
        ii. "Misapplication" – The rite is applied to inappropriate persons or circumstances
    B. "Misexecutions" – Act vitiated
        i. "Flaw" – Incorrect, vague, or inexplicit formula
        ii. "Hitch" – Incomplete Procedure
2. "Ineffectuality" – Act fails to precipitate change
3. "Contagion" – Act leaps beyond proper boundaries
4. "Opacity" – Act unrecognizable or unintelligible
5. "Omission" – Act not performed

6. "Misframe" – Genre of act misconstrued
7. "Defeat" – Act discredits or invalidates the acts of others
8. "Violation" – Act effective, but demeaning
9. "Abuse" – Act professed but hollow

   A. "Insincerity" – Lack of requisite feelings, thoughts, or orientation
   B. "Breach" – Failure to follow through
   C. "Gloss" – Procedures to cover up flaws
   D. "Flop" – Failure to produce appropriate mood or atmosphere

Ritual Mitigation of Infelicitous Performance

No matter who we are, we will often find ourselves faced with the reality of a ritual "gone wrong." It is important to realize that there are resolutions that can be taken.

If you realize that something went wrong during the rite, a **piacular offering** is not uncommon. This is an offering made, usually at the discretion of the priest in charge, to resolve any of the above issues during the rite (in an ADF rite, this would come after the Prayer of Sacrifice).

If you realize after the rite that something has gone wrong, an **expiation rite** may be performed. This is a rite that resolves whatever issue was brought up. Most Pagan priests are trained in this sort of ritual and can lend a hand if something is not right.

If you feel that you did more than one thing wrong, there is always what might be best termed the **mulligan rite**, or a "do-over" rite, where you do everything all over again. You may wish to make a piacular offering as part of this rite, even if everything seems to be going right.

It is rare that you will find yourself in a real bind for an infelicitous performance, but remember that there are plenty of options. Also, remember that sacred time is a special, strange thing: if you somehow flubbed your Beltaine rite but don't realize it until Lughnassadh, *you can still re-do your Beltaine rite!* There really is no rule that would prevent that in modern Pagansim.

Recipes From Skarlett

One of the key things we learned in the feedback from the workshops we did in Feb. 2012 was that Skarlett, our own amazing kitchen witch, is an amazing cook. We got so many compliments on the food that we decided to provide the recipes for the meat pies she made that day! So, here are the two key recipes for your enjoyment!

Chicken-Cheddar Potato Pie

Ingredients:

- 3 chicken-apple sausages
- 1 cup apple juice
- ¾ cup water
- pinch of Herbs de Provence
- 4 cups mashed potatoes
- 1 cup shredded sharp cheddar
- fresh cracked black pepper
- 1 teaspoon granulated garlic
- 2 big pinches Herbs de Provence
- 1 package of pie crust
- chicken bouillon
- a handful of beans

Pre-heat oven to 350° F. Slice the sausages into half-inch rounds and poach in apple juice, water and a pinch of herbs de Provence for 20 minutes. Line a pie plate with pie crust, tamp it down, flute the edges and scatter beans on the bottom. Place pie crust in oven for seven minutes, then take out and discard the beans. Prepare instant mashed potatoes according to box instructions, but instead of the water commonly used in preparation, use chicken bouillon. While making the potatoes, season with pepper, garlic and Herbs de Provence.

While the potatoes are hot, stir in the cheese. Strain the sausage out of the apple juice and then mix the rounds into the potatoes. Fill the pie crust with potato-sausage mixture and then place in the oven for 15-20 minutes. Take out and let cool 10 minutes and then serve. Makes one pie.

Spiced Meat Pie

• 1 package of pie crust • 1 egg • ¼ cup water • 2 pounds ground beef • 1¼ cup beef stock • ¼ cup apple juice • 1 cup dried cranberries • 1 large chopped onion	• ½ teaspoon sea salt • ¼ teaspoon granulated garlic • ¼ teaspoon fresh cracked black pepper • 2 pinches Herbs de Provence • 1½ teaspoons Pumpkin Pie Spice

Pre-heat oven to 500° F. Beat egg and water together. Line a pie plate with a pie crust tamp it down, flute the edges and then brush crust with the egg mixture. Place stock, juice, meat, onion, cranberries and seasonings and blend them into a large sauce pan.

Place pan on stove and bring filling to a boil, then turn the heat down and let simmer 30-40 minutes, stirring frequently so it does not scorch. Once cooked, spoon filling into pie crust with a slotted spoon. Top with second pie crust, seal and crimp the edges and poke crust with a fork in several places to create vents. Brush top crust with egg mixture and place in oven. Bake at 500° for 10 minutes, then turn oven down to 375° and bake 20 more minutes. Take out of oven and set aside to cool 15 minutes, slice and then serve.

Further Reading

Bell, Catherine. *Ritual: Perspectives and Dimensions*. New York: Oxford University Press, 1997. Print.

Dangler, Michael. *A Crane Breviary and Guide Book: Rituals for the Cranes of ADF, When They Must Kindle Their Own Good Fire*. Columbus, OH: Garanus Publishing, 2011. Print.

Dangler, Michael, ed. *The Fire On Our Hearth: A Devotional of Three Cranes Grove, ADF*. Columbus, OH: Garanus Publishing, 2010. Print.

Dangler, Michael and James Dillard. *The Call of the Crane: A Working Guide for Members of the ADF Order of the Crane*. Columbus, OH: Garanus Publishing, 2009. Print.

Goodman, Felicitas and Nauwald, Nana. *Ecstatic Trance: New Ritual Body Postures: A Workbook*. Holland: Binkey Kok Publications, 2003. Print

Grimes, Ronald. *Beginnings in Ritual Studies*. Waterloo, CA: Ritual Studies International, 2010. Print

---. *Ritual Criticism: Case Studies in Its Practice, Essays on Its Theories*. Waterloo, CA: Ritual Studies International, 2010. Print

Stanislavski, Constantin. *An Actor Prepares*. Trans. Hapgood, Elizabeth Reynolds. New York: Theatre Arts Books, 1948. Print.

Thomas, Kirk. "Concentration In Ritual." *Ár nDraíocht Féin: A Druid Fellowship*. ADF, December 22, 2009. PDF file. <http://www.adf.org/rituals/explanations/Concentration-In-Ritual.pdf>

---. "The Well-Trained Ritualist." *Ár nDraíocht Féin: A Druid Fellowship*. ADF, December 22, 2009. PDF file. < http://www.adf.org/rituals/explanations/Well-Trained-Ritualist.pdf>

Pagan Fire Seminars

Interested in a Pagan Fire Seminar for your Grove or ritual working group? Please contact us at info@magicaldruid.com for more information!

The Magical Druid

Your one-stop shop for ritual gear, herbs, and magical supplies! Visit us at

http://www.magicaldruid.com/

Interested in Druidry?

Check out Ár nDraíocht Féin: A Druid Fellowship (ADF) at

http://www.adf.org/

May you pray with a good fire!

www.ingramcontent.com/pod-product-compliance
Lightning Source LLC
LaVergne TN
LVHW051840080426
835512LV00018B/2993